In Our Hands

IN OUR HANDS

A Plan to Replace the Welfare State

Charles Murray

THE AEI PRESS

Publisher for the American Enterprise Institute
WASHINGTON, D.C.

To the memory of Joan Kennedy Taylor,
who opened the way

Distributed to the Trade by National Book Network, 15200 NBN Way, Blue Ridge Summit, PA 17214. To order call toll free 1-800-462-6420 or 1-717-794-3800. For all other inquiries please contact the AEI Press, 1150 Seventeenth Street, NW, Washington, DC 20036 or call 1-800-862-5801.

Library of Congress Cataloging-in-Publication Data
Murray, Charles A.
  In our hands : a plan to replace the welfare state / Charles Murray.
    p. cm.
Includes bibliographical references and index.

  ISBN-10 0-8447-4223-6 (cloth: alk. paper)
  ISBN-13 978-0-8447-4223-6

  1. United States—Social policy—1993—Economic aspects.
2. Guaranteed annual income—United States. 3. Negative income tax—United States. 4. Public welfare—United States—Finance.
5. Welfare state—United States. I. American Enterprise Institute for Public Policy Research. II. Title.

  HN65.M85 2006
  361.6'80973—dc22

                                                        2005030558

  10 09 08 07 06   1 2 3 4 5

© 2006 by the American Enterprise Institute for Public Policy Research, Washington, D.C. All rights reserved. No part of this publication may be used or reproduced in any manner whatsoever without permission in writing from the American Enterprise Institute except in the case of brief quotations embodied in news articles, critical articles, or reviews. The views expressed in the publications of the American Enterprise Institute are those of the authors and do not necessarily reflect the views of the staff, advisory panels, officers, or trustees of AEI.

Printed in the United States of America

Contents

List of Illustrations

Acknowledgments

In Our Hands is dedicated to Joan Kennedy Taylor, who, in the autumn of 1982, phoned me from out of the blue. She told me she was the director of publications at the Manhattan Institute, and asked whether I was interested in expanding an article I had written for *The Public Interest* into a book. I was, and the book became *Losing Ground.* My gratitude goes as well to William Hammett, the Manhattan Institute's president, who had also read the article and encouraged Joan to get hold of me. His young institute was operating on a shoestring in those days, but Bill found a way to get me a $33,000 advance on royalties and thereby made the project possible.

Twenty-one years later, I got another call from out of the blue, this one from my old friend Irwin Stelzer, who informed me that he knew the title of my next book even though he didn't know what would be in it. I had been writing about social problems for long enough that it was time for me to write my own *What Is To Be Done*, Irwin said, following in Lenin's footsteps.

Irwin had inspired a book idea once before, for *Human Accomplishment*, a book so difficult and exhausting to write that I instinctively recoiled from any new plan he had in mind for me. But as it happened, I did have something I wanted to say about policy solutions. I am a libertarian, but for many years I had thought there ought to be some way to extend a hand across the political divide between libertarians and social democrats, offering a compromise that provided generous assistance for dealing with human needs without entailing the suffocating and soulless welfare state. Milton Friedman's concept of a negative income tax (NIT) appealed to me as the basis for that compromise. In the late 1980s, I had even written a draft of an article laying out a plan for a revised NIT, but put it away because I could not design it as I wished and still make it affordable. As I reconsidered the issue in 2003, I realized that the intervening years had given the government a lot more money to work with. The technical problems that had vexed me in the late 1980s could be solved.

Thanks go to colleagues at the American Enterprise Institute who read drafts and offered help of many kinds, chief among them Chris DeMuth, Joe Antos, Doug Besharov, Karlyn Bowman, Nick Eberstadt, and Kevin Hassett. Wilson Taylor and Stephen Hyde contributed their specialized expertises to the chapter on health care. Two experts on Social Security, Andrew Biggs and Derrick Max, helped me navigate the rocks and shoals of that daunting system. John Skar contributed his actuarial expertise to an overall review of the numbers. Sam Thernstrom and Lisa Parmelee contributed meticulous editorial assistance and inspired many improvements to the text.

Policy scholars John Cogan, Sheldon Danziger, and Robert Haveman read the penultimate draft and offered critiques from their varying perspectives. Their criticisms prompted dozens of revisions, a few thousand words of new text, and a new appendix—improvements all, though not ones that will reconcile them to an approach that they reject. Sheldon and Bob, who are good social democrats, have my particular thanks for their collegiality in a polarized age. As in all of my endeavors, I must emphasize that just because someone has helped me with my work does not imply endorsement of any part of the result.

Sitting at a desk beside me when I took that call from Joan Taylor in 1982 was my new girlfriend, Catherine Cox. As I write, she is sitting at a desk about fifty feet away from me—now wife, mother of our children, and my most demanding editor. But not even an editor as brilliant as she can give me the words to express the love I feel.

CHARLES MURRAY
Burkittsville, Maryland
November 1, 2005

Ground Rules

An old joke has three men stuck at the bottom of a hole, each presenting his plan to escape. I have forgotten who the first two are, but the third is an economist. When his turn comes he begins by saying, "First, we assume a ladder."

This book puts me in the position of the economist. The ladder I will be describing to you would work if it existed, but today's American politicians will not build it. I must ask you to suspend disbelief and play along.

My part of the bargain is to be realistic about everything else, presenting evidence that the policy is financially feasible and would produce the desirable results I claim—not in a utopia, but in the United States of the twenty-first century.

In short, the ground rules are that I am free to ignore that my thought experiment will not soon become policy, but I must demonstrate that it should. Perhaps someone more resourceful than I will devise variations that can be turned into law.

Introduction

A Short Statement of the Argument

America's population is wealthier than any in history. Every year, the American government redistributes more than a trillion dollars of that wealth to provide for retirement, health care, and the alleviation of poverty. We still have millions of people without comfortable retirements, without adequate health care, and living in poverty. Only a government can spend so much money so ineffectually. The solution is to give the money to the people.

A Longer Statement of the Argument

The European and American welfare states evolved under the twin assumptions that resources were scarce and that government could allocate them effectively.

1

The first assumption was true during the first half of the twentieth century, in this sense: No country had ever been so rich that its wealth, divided evenly among everyone, would provide everyone with a comfortable living.

After World War II, in a few countries, wealth increased so much that, for the first time in human history, there was enough money to go around. It was technically possible for no one to be poor. Much of the energy behind the social turmoil of the 1960s was fueled by this revolutionary change.

Enter the second of the assumptions, that governments could allocate resources effectively. During the early decades of the welfare state, it seemed simple. The indigent elderly depend on charity, so let the government provide everyone with a guaranteed pension. The unemployed husband and father cannot find a job, so let the government give him some useful work to do and pay him for it. Some people who are sick cannot afford to go to a private physician, so let the government pay for health care.

It turned out not to be simple after all. The act of giving pensions increased the probability that people reached old age needing them. Governments had a hard time finding useful work for unemployed people and were ineffectual employers even when they did. The demand for medical care outstripped the supply. But, despite the complications, these were the easy tasks. Scandinavia and the Netherlands—small, ethnically homogeneous societies, with traditions of work, thrift, neighborliness, and social consensus—did them best.

Traditions decay when the reality facing the new generation changes. The habit of thrift decays if there is no penalty for not saving. The work ethic decays if there is no penalty for not working. Neighborliness decays when neighbors are no longer needed. Social consensus decays with immigration. Even the easy tasks became hard as time went on.

During the second half of the twentieth century, the welfare state confronted accelerating increases in the number of people who were not just poor, but who behaved in destructive ways that ensured they would remain poor, sometimes living off their fellow citizens, sometimes preying on them. As their numbers grew, they acquired a new name: the underclass. The underclass grew first in the nation that was the largest and ethnically most heterogeneous: the United States. As the years passed, poor young men increasingly reached adulthood unprepared to work even when jobs were available. They were more disposed to commit crimes. Poor young women more often bore children without a husband. Poor children more often were born to parents who were incompetent to nurture them. When it came to solving these problems, it was obvious by the 1980s that government had failed. Then the evidence grew that government had exacerbated the problems it was trying to solve. As the Americans were making these discoveries, an underclass also began to emerge in the European welfare states.

That the easy tasks of the welfare state became hard and that underclasses are growing throughout the Western world are neither coincidences nor inevitable byproducts of modernity. The welfare state produces its own destruction. The process takes decades to play out, but it is inexorable. First, the welfare state degrades the traditions of work, thrift, and neighborliness that enabled a society to work at the outset; then it spawns social and economic problems that it is powerless to solve. The welfare state as we have come to know it is everywhere within decades of financial and social bankruptcy.

The libertarian solution is to prevent the government from redistributing money in the first place. Imagine for a moment that the trillion-plus dollars that the United States government spends on transfer payments were left instead in the hands of the people who started with them. If I could wave a magic wand, that would be my solution. It is a case I have made elsewhere.[1] Leave the wealth where it originates, and watch how its many uses, individual and collaborative, enable civil society to meet the needs that government cannot.

But that is a solution that upwards of 90 percent of the population will dismiss. Some will dismiss it because they do not accept that people will behave in the cooperative and compassionate ways that I believe they would. But there is another sticking point for many people with which I am sympathetic: People are unequal in the abilities that lead to economic success in life.

To the extent that inequality of wealth is grounded in the way people freely choose to conduct their lives, I do not find it troubling. People are complicated bundles of skills and motivations, strengths and weaknesses, and so are their roads to happiness. Some people pursue happiness in ways that tend to be accompanied by large incomes, others in ways that tend to be accompanied by lower incomes. In a free society, these choices are made voluntarily, with psychic rewards balanced against monetary rewards. Income inequality is accordingly large. So what?

Inequality of wealth grounded in unequal abilities is different. For most of us, the luck of the draw cuts several ways—one person is not handsome, but is smart; another is not as smart, but is industrious; still another is not as industrious, but is charming. This kind of inequality of human capital is enriching, making life more interesting for everyone. But some portion of the population gets the short end of the stick on several dimensions. As the number of dimensions grows, so does the punishment for being unlucky. When a society tries to redistribute the goods of life to compensate the most unlucky, its heart is in the right place, however badly the thing has worked out in practice.

Hence this book. The argument starts by accepting that the American government will continue to spend a huge amount of money on income transfers. It then contends that we should take all of that money and give it back to the American people in cash grants. The chapters that follow explain how it might be done, why it is economically feasible, and the good that would follow.

PART I

Framework

1

The Plan

A year after the end of World War II, an economist from the University of Chicago named George Stigler, later a Nobel laureate, wrote an article criticizing the minimum wage as a way of combating poverty. In passing, he mentioned an idea that had been suggested to him by a young colleague, also a future Nobel laureate, Milton Friedman: Instead of raising the minimum wage or trying to administer complicated welfare systems, just give poor people the cash difference between what they make and the income necessary for a decent standard of living. The idea came to be called a negative income tax, or NIT.[1]

In the early 1960s, Friedman formally proposed the NIT as a replacement for all income transfers.[2] A few years later Robert Lampman, a scholar of the left, also endorsed it, and a political constituency for experimenting with the NIT began to grow.[3] During the 1970s, the federal government sponsored test versions of the NIT in selected sites in Iowa,

New Jersey, Indiana, Pennsylvania, and, most ambitiously, in Denver and Seattle.

The experimental NIT produced disappointing results. The work disincentives were substantial and ominously largest among the youngest recipients. Marital breakup was higher among participants than among the control group in most of the sites.[4] No headlines announced these results, but the NIT quietly disappeared from the policy debate.

Though the NIT of the experiment was nothing like Friedman's idea—it augmented the existing transfer payments instead of replacing them—it did convincingly demonstrate that a simple floor on income is a bad idea. There is no incentive to work at jobs that pay less than the floor, and the marginal tax rates on jobs that pay a little more than the floor are punishingly high. But as the amounts of money that the United States spent on the poor continued to soar during the 1980s and 1990s, while poverty remained as high as it had been since the early 1970s, the underlying appeal of the NIT persisted: If we're spending that much money to eradicate poverty, why not just give poor people enough cash so that they won't be poor, and be done with it?[5]

Friedman's concept was valid. The devil was in the details. A variant of the NIT puts it within our power to end poverty, provide for comfortable retirement and medical care for everyone, and, as a bonus that is probably more important than any of the immediate effects, to revitalize American civil society.

The Plan—I have not been able to contrive a better name for it—converts all transfer payments to a single cash payment for everyone age twenty-one and older. It would require a constitutional amendment that I am not competent to frame in legal language, but its sense is easy to express:

> Henceforth, federal, state, and local governments shall make no law nor establish any program that provides benefits to some citizens but not to others. All programs currently providing such benefits are to be terminated. The funds formerly allocated to them are to be used instead to provide every citizen with a cash grant beginning at age twenty-one and continuing until death. The annual value of the cash grant at the program's outset is to be $10,000.

The Plan does not require much in the way of bureaucratic apparatus. Its administration consists of computerized electronic deposits to bank accounts, plus resources to identify fraud. Here are the nuts and bolts:

- *Universal passport.* At the time of the Plan's adoption, each U.S. citizen receives a passport that has the same official status and uses as the current passport. Subsequently, a passport is issued to each U.S. citizen at birth. This passport also establishes eligibility for the grant.

- *A bank account.* A condition of receiving the grant is that the citizen notify the government of an account at any United States financial institution with an American Bankers Association (ABA) routing number. The grant is electronically deposited into the account monthly.[6] No bank account, no grant.

One Step at a Time

Describing the Plan in the language of a constitutional amendment raises a host of practical questions. For example, how would local and state expenditures on transfer programs be captured to fund the Plan? It would be an important question if we were about to have a congressional debate on an actual constitutional amendment. But we are stellar distances away from that point. In this instance, the limited proposition I defend is that we are spending so much money on transfers that the Plan will surely be affordable by the time it could become a live political issue. Let's begin by thinking about whether that proposition is true.

The same distinction will recur throughout the book, as I focus on the question, "Is this doable if we want it badly enough?" while ignoring problems that would need to be worked out if we got to the point of debating the Plan in Congress. Unless people who care about social policy are willing to do this, the solutions we can consider will always amount to tinkering.

• *Reimbursement schedule.* Earned income has no effect on the grant until that income reaches $25,000. From $25,000 to $50,000, a surtax is levied that reimburses the grant up to a maximum of $5,000. The surtax is 20 percent of incremental earned income (e.g., the tax at $30,000 is 20 percent of $30,000 – $25,000, or $1,000). Appendix C shows the tax rates and after-tax income for

various income levels under the current system and
the Plan.

- *Eligibility.* The definition of earned income is based
  on individuals regardless of marital status or living
  arrangements. Thus, a wife who makes less than
  $25,000 will get the full $10,000 no matter how
  much her husband makes.

- *Changes in the size of the grant.* As time goes on, even
  low inflation will erode the purchasing power of the
  grant. One option is to link its size to median personal earned income.[7] Another is for Congress to
  make ad hoc adjustments to it, and a third is to link
  it to inflation. I leave the provision for adjusting the
  size of the grant open. The government's projections
  of the costs and benefits of maintaining the current
  system customarily assume zero inflation, and so will
  my projections of the costs and benefits of the Plan.

- *Tax revenues.* The calculations assume that the tax
  system continues to generate revenue at the current
  rate without specifying how the tax code might be
  changed. Whether current Social Security and Medicare taxes should remain as they are, or whether the
  amounts of money they generate should be folded
  into individual or corporate taxes, are separate issues
  that I do not try to address.

- *The programs to be eliminated.* The Plan eliminates
  programs that are unambiguously transfers—Social
  Security, Medicare, Medicaid, welfare programs, social
  service programs, agricultural subsidies, and corporate welfare. It does not apply a strict libertarian

Transfers Contrasted with Public Goods Classically Defined

The benefits that a government provides to the governed span a range from public goods classically defined at one extreme to pure transfers at the other, with *transfer* meaning benefits that are bestowed only on some citizens, groups, or organizations.

Public goods classically defined are ones that are available to everyone on equal terms, and that can be consumed by one citizen without making the good less available to another. The purest examples are national defense, police protection, and, in more recent times, clean air.

Benefits that are bestowed only on some citizens, groups, or organizations can be defended as public goods in a loose sense ("It is good for a society as a whole if the homeless are given shelter," or "It is good for a society as a whole if the family farm is protected"), but they are qualitatively different from classic public goods. The immediate benefit (shelter for the homeless, an agricultural subsidy) goes to certain identifiable individuals and not to others. Furthermore, two citizens cannot jointly share the good as they can jointly share national defense or clean air. The bed I occupy in the homeless shelter means one less bed available for everyone else. When a farmer gets his subsidy check, that money cannot be used for any other farmer. Following common usage, I label these benefits *transfers*. Tax dollars are taken from some citizens and given to others in cash, kind, or services. Whether the transfers are justified is not at issue at the moment, merely the fact that they are transfers.

definition of transfer, leaving activities such as state-funded education, funding for transportation infra-structure, and the postal service in place.[8] A complete list of the programs that the Plan replaces is given in appendix A.

That's the Plan. A cash grant, with a surtax, funded by eliminating the transfers that currently exist. I will later pro-pose additional reforms pertaining to health care, but the Plan could be implemented without them. I will also note that some legal restrictions on how the recipient uses the grant could be introduced. But I will argue that many of the best effects of the Plan are fostered by the least direction: "Here's the money. Use it as you see fit. Your life is in your hands."

2

Basic Finances

A guaranteed minimum income of $10,000 a year for every adult American citizen is financially within our reach. By about 2011 it will be cheaper than maintaining the system we have in place. I will work through the individual steps leading to that conclusion, but a good place to begin is by realizing how much the United States spends on transfers. In 2002, the year that will be the benchmark for all the financial calculations in this book, the expenditures on the programs to be replaced by the Plan already amounted to the equivalent of about $6,900 for every man and woman in the United States age twenty-one or older. As I write in 2005, we are somewhere over the $7,000 mark and rising fast.

Now to work through the arithmetic more systematically, using constant 2002 dollars unless I specify otherwise.

The Cost of the Plan in 2002

Eligible population. In 2002, the resident population of the United States ages twenty-one and older was estimated to be 202.3 million persons.[1] About 7 million—immigrants who are not citizens and incarcerated criminals—would not be eligible for the grant.[2] I do not correct the projected costs of the Plan for them. This is the first example of a principle applied for the rest of the book: When projecting the costs of the Plan, err on the high side; when calculating and projecting the costs of the current system, err on the low side. The result is that my conclusions about the financial feasibility of the Plan have a cushion. Appendix E lists the many applications of the principle. In this first instance, I project the gross cost of the Plan if it had been implemented in 2002 at $2.023 trillion, overstating its cost by about $70 billion.

Reimbursement. Under the Plan, the grant begins to be paid back through a surtax at $25,000 of earned income. People making $50,000 or more pay back half of the grant through the surtax. As of 2002, 36.6 million individuals with income made $50,000 or more.[3] They reduce the net cost of the program by $183 billion. Assume that individuals making from $25,000 to $50,000 pay back an average of $1,794 of the grant.[4] There were 56.0 million such people, reducing the net cost by an additional $100 billion.[5] This leaves $1.74 trillion as the initial cost of the program if it had been implemented in 2002.

Expenditures on programs that the Plan replaces. The Plan replaces three categories of programs: means-tested programs, income-transfer programs that are not means-tested, and a category that I will label "transfers to industry, nonprofits, and favored groups."

The means-tested programs to be eliminated are defined by the table in the *Statistical Abstract of the United States* entitled, "Cash and Noncash Benefits for Persons with Limited Income." They include such major programs as Medicaid, supplemental security income, the earned income tax credit, food stamps, and temporary assistance for needy families. A full list of the programs is given in appendix A. Total expenditures for 2002, combining federal with state and local, was $522 billion.[6]

The other income-transfer programs to be replaced by the Plan are Social Security, Medicare, unemployment insurance, and the government's payments to workers' compensation. In 2002, expenditures on these programs amounted to $800 billion.[7]

I estimate expenditures on transfers to corporations, groups, and favored individuals at $63 billion in 2002.[8] By far the biggest category is agricultural subsidies. A list of these programs is also shown in appendix A. This number is far too small. For reasons explained in the note, it ignores at least a few hundred billion dollars spent on transfers by states, counties, and municipalities.[9]

In all, the expenditures on programs to be replaced amounted to $1.385 trillion in 2002, compared to the Plan's residual funding requirement of $1.740 trillion. In other words, as of 2002, the Plan could have been implemented with a $355 billion shortfall.[10]

Making Up the Shortfall

I will not bother to consider ways of closing that gap through increased taxation or additional budget cuts, because the gap will disappear on its own in a few years, for two reasons.

First, increases in the cost of the Plan will be much smaller than increases in the cost of the current system. The cost of the Plan will increase as the population increases and ages.[11] The cost projections described in appendix B take these demographic changes into account. But one of the attractive features of the Plan is that cost projections are not subject to big surprises (we already have a very accurate idea of what the population will look like over the next few decades), and we can be confident that the increase in costs will be only about 1 percent per year—not in per-capita spending, but total spending.[12] Total government spending on the programs the Plan replaces will rise much faster. We know that to be true because of history and demography.

History tells us that from 1980 to 2000, the annual real increase in the costs of the programs to be replaced averaged 2.9 percent, almost three times the rate of increase for the Plan.[13] Demography tells us that the aging Baby Boomers are about to generate increases in Social Security and Medicare far larger than those we saw in 1980–2000. Many analyses of this issue have been conducted, because the looming budget problem it represents rightly preoccupies today's budget planners. I have employed the budget projections prepared by the U.S. Congressional Budget Office (CBO).[14] The CBO projections for Social Security work out to an annual average increase of 3.6 percent, and the projections for Medicare work out to an annual average increase of 7.2 percent, compared to the annual 1 percent increase in the cost of the Plan.

The second reason for the disappearance of the gap is that the upper part of the income distribution keeps getting fatter. As of 2002, the median income of all people with incomes was $22,118. After adding in those without incomes, most people would have gotten the entire $10,000 grant as of 2002.[15] But if more and more people pay back more and more of the grant as the years go by, the per-capita costs of the Plan will decrease.

History gives us reason to expect this happy outcome. Between 1970 and 2001, the percentage of people with income who made $50,000 or more (in constant 2001 dollars for this time series) more than doubled, from 8.3 percent to 17.7 percent.[16] Furthermore, we can expect this percentage to increase even if median income is stagnant. The reason for this counterintuitive conclusion lies in the difference between a median and a mean. The median income of $22,118 as of 2002 says only that half of people with incomes made more than that amount. It does not say how much more. The issue when projecting the costs of the Plan is how income is distributed within the upper half of the distribution. An example will illustrate. Between 1970 and 1990, real male median income scarcely budged, growing by a total of only

1.2 percent. But during that same twenty years, the proportion of men with income who earned $50,000 or more (in constant 2001 dollars) rose by 43 percent.[17] The percentage of people who pay back the maximum surtax can be expected to grow over time, even assuming zero inflation and even if median income is stagnant.[18]

Figure 1 pulls together the strands of this discussion by showing the projected costs of the Plan versus continuation of the current system.

FIGURE 1

PROJECTED COSTS OF THE CURRENT SYSTEM AND THE PLAN

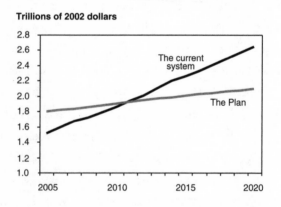

SOURCE: Author's calculations from data in appendix B.

The projection of costs for the current system (black line in the graph) uses a combination of budget forecasts by the Congressional Budget Office and extrapolations from past expenditures, described in appendix B. The projection of the costs of the Plan (gray line), also described in appendix B, uses census projections for population by sex and age, applied to the income distribution by sex and age as of 2002. This projection assumes that the income distribution will remain unchanged—an upper bound for the cost of the Plan.[19]

The projected costs of the current system and of the Plan cross in 2011. By 2020, the Plan would cost $549 billion less than a continuation of the current system—again, projecting no increase whatsoever in the percentage of people making $50,000 or more. This statement does not take transition costs into account—but, on the other hand, a system that promises to cost half a trillion dollars less than the current system *per year* by 2020 leaves a lot of wiggle room for dealing with transition costs. Appendix D discusses the financial tradeoffs for the affluent and ways of dealing with transition costs.

This overview of finances leaves other loose ends. Appendix B elaborates on details that I have skipped here; chapter 7 takes up the question of work disincentives and presents the reasons for thinking they would be acceptable. But it is important to begin with the basics of the arithmetic:

- The amount that this nation already spends and is committed to spending on transfers is huge and rising fast.

- Divide these huge, rising amounts by the number of people over twenty-one, and a $10,000-per-year grant is easily within reach within a few years. By 2020, it can be expected to cost about half a trillion dollars less per year than the current system.

- This comparison between the Plan and the current system holds true even when unrealistically conservative assumptions are made in calculating the present and future costs of the Plan.

Holding those thoughts in mind, it is time to consider what the Plan would accomplish.

PART II

Immediate Effects

3

Retirement

The next five chapters explore the immediate effects of the Plan on retirement, health care, poverty, the underclass, and work disincentives. I begin with retirement, at the forefront of the continuing debate over the future of Social Security.

Most people are aware that Social Security is a bad deal as an investment, but a widespread impression persists that at least Social Security provides a floor for everyone that has nearly eliminated poverty among the elderly. Social Security does not accomplish even that much. As of 2002, 3.6 million elderly Americans were below the poverty line—more than one out of every ten people ages sixty-five and older, a rate only slightly lower than the poverty rate for the overall population.[1] A total of 5.8 million elderly people, one out of six, had incomes below 125 percent of the poverty line.[2]

Social Security can leave so many people so poor because it is not universal and because the benefits for people who have worked only a portion of their adult lives are well below the poverty line. This leaves women who spend most of their lives as mothers and housewives in a precarious position. A woman gets no survivor benefits via a divorced husband's employment record unless the marriage lasted ten years. She gets no benefits unless she has worked ten years or more. A middle-aged woman who gets a low-paying job after her divorce and does work more than ten years usually does not have time to qualify for benefits that keep her out of poverty in old age.[3] Thus the first significant advantage of the Plan over the current system: It is universal, and even in the worst case provides $10,000 a year for every elderly person in the country.

But the Plan does more than give everyone a guaranteed income floor. The Plan makes it possible for low-income people to have a comfortable retirement, not just get by. Take the case of a twenty-one-year-old who is going into the labor force and will be steadily employed at a low-income job all his life—he will always make $20,000 per year, let us say. If you go to the Social Security Administration's web page for calculating benefits and enter these assumptions, you will be told that this young person can expect a monthly Social Security payment of $916 in today's dollars, or an annual income of $10,992.[4] That is almost precisely the poverty line for an elderly two-person household as of 2002 ($10,885), and about $2,400 more than the poverty line for a one-person household ($8,628).[5]

That meager Social Security benefit will have been created by forty-five years of payroll tax payments.[6] As of 2005, the amount of that payment for a man making $20,000 was $2,480 annually.[7] Now suppose that our young worker puts the same $2,480 into a mutual fund indexed to some broadly based measure of the stock market and continues doing so for forty-five years. Assuming a return of 4 percent compounded annually, the value of his holdings when he retires will be $300,153. If you go to an annuities calculator web page and enter these data, you will be told that our low-income worker will be able to buy a lifetime annuity paying $24,350 annually.[8] Because his retirement income is less than $25,000, he will continue to get all of the $10,000 grant, for a total annual income of $34,350. Compare this to the annual income of $10,992 he can expect from the current system, and the discrepancy is striking. He will have to pay for his medical care on his own, because Medicare will have disappeared. I take up health care in the next chapter; for now, I will observe that he can buy a lot of medical coverage with the extra $23,358.

The 4 Percent Assumption

The first issue is whether my projection of a 4 percent real annual return is realistic. It is, in fact, conservative, far below the expectation of a 7 percent average real yield used by the Advisory Council to the Social Security Administration (SSA) in 1994–96, the 6.5 percent expectation used by the SSA in analyzing the three models for modifying Social Security that were presented to the President's Commission to Strengthen Social Security in 2001, or the 6.8 percent used by the Congressional Budget Office in analyzing the work of the commission.[9] But because a realistic estimate of annual return is so central to so many aspects of the Plan, an extended discussion of the 4 percent assumption is appropriate, along with a response to those who argue that relying on such returns in the future is too risky.

Risk and return to various types of investments and investment strategies are not matters of opinion. The data are voluminous, available from many countries, and sometimes extend back for centuries. Economist Jeremy Siegel has used such data to compile histories of real returns to alternative financial instruments in the United States, the United Kingdom, Germany, and Japan. Siegel's data for the United States from 1802 to 2001 are shown in figure 2 on the following page.[10] Note that the scale on the vertical axis is logarithmic, visually understating the level of growth but making it easier to inspect the percentage changes in the markets. Equal vertical distances represent equal percentage changes in return throughout the chart.

Stocks have been by far the best investment in two ways. First, the return to stocks during the two centuries covered by the graph has been orders of magnitude larger than the return from bonds (gold is not even worth considering). Second, the long-term return to stocks has been more reliable than returns to the other investments. Over the course of American history, an investor who left his money alone for three or four decades could not fail to make a substantial profit if he invested in a broad-based portfolio of stocks, whereas it was possible to have low or even negative yields for gold or bonds over similar periods.

FIGURE 2

TOTAL REAL RETURN INDEXES, 1802–2001

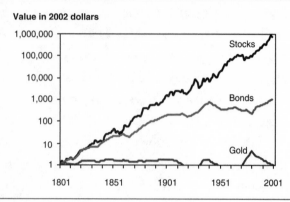

Value in 2002 dollars

SOURCE: Siegel (1998), fig. 1-4, updated to 2001.

Let us apply the story from figure 2 to my assumption that the low-income worker will get an average real return of 4 percent compounded annually over the forty-five-year period from the time he is twenty-one until he retires.[11] Figure 3 shows the average real return over every forty-five-year period from 1801–46 to 1956–2001.

As the figure indicates, the average return over a forty-five-year period has only occasionally dipped below 6 percent. The average over all such periods is 7 percent. But when talking about retirement, the issue for many people is not averages. People are worried about worst cases. Thus, the bursting of the stock market bubble in 2001 provided politicians and editorial writers with material for attacking plans to privatize Social Security.

Figure 3 lends perspective. The forty-five-year average annual return for a market-based portfolio did drop

FIGURE 3

FORTY-FIVE-YEAR COMPOUND AVERAGE GROWTH
RATE FOR THE STOCK MARKET

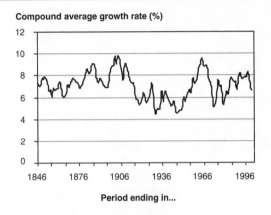

SOURCE: Siegel (1998), fig. 1-4 updated to 2001.

abruptly in 2001—but it still remained at more than 6 percent. The same perspective applies to much worse dips in the markets. Suppose, for example, that you were unlucky enough to have invested every cent of your retirement nest egg at the peak of the market in 1929 before the Great Depression. At the end of the forty-five-year period, in 1974, whatever you put in would have increased in value more than eightfold—an average annual compounded return of about 4.9 percent.

Suppose that you had suffered the unluckiest timing in American history: Your forty-five-year period began in 1887, you invested all of your money in that year, and you had to withdraw it to buy your retirement annuity in 1932 at the bottom of the Great Depression. In that case—literally the worst case—your nest egg would have grown about seven-fold and your average return would still have been about 4.3 percent. My estimated 4 percent annual real return over forty-five years assumes that everyone's timing will always be worse than the unluckiest investors in American history.[12]

Frequently Asked Questions

No matter how decisive the data on long-term returns from the stock market may be, many readers will not like the idea of letting people manage their own retirement plans without the backstop of Social Security. Here are my responses to the most common objections I have heard.

What about people who don't put anything away or invest their money unwisely? A familiar argument for preferring Social Security to a privatized version is that Social Security ensures an income floor for everyone, no matter how improvident or how incompetent an investor a person might be. They are wrong about "everyone," as I discussed at the opening of the chapter. More to the point of this question, the Plan *does* provide a universal floor. Everyone, including the improvident and incompetent who have squandered everything, still have $10,000 a year each, $20,000 for a couple, no matter what. Six people who have completely squandered everything can pool their resources and have $60,000 per year; and so on. If a guaranteed floor is important to you, the Plan does a far better job than the current system.[13]

But squandering everything is the worst case. The broader question is whether ordinary people can be expected to plan for their own retirements and invest their money wisely, to which my short answer is: Why not? The large retirement income that I produced from a working income of $20,000 a year is based on the same amount that people at that income level are currently required by law to save for retirement. Accumulating that sum does not require people to make sophisticated investment choices; it is based on the result if they buy a fund based on a broad market index and leave it alone during a hypothesized worst investment period in American history. For that matter, obtaining a 4 percent return does not require investing exclusively in equities. The CBO analysis of the President's Commission to Strengthen Social Security projects an average real return of 5.2 percent from a portfolio consisting of 50 percent equities, 20 percent treasury bonds, and 30 percent corporate bonds.[14]

The question then becomes, how many people will take advantage of this easily available strategy? There is one simple solution: Require everyone to take advantage of it. If the only reason you oppose the Plan is that you are worried about people doing foolish things with their money, continue the legal compulsion and restrict the investment choices. The Plan could be modified to stipulate that some percentage of the grant be deposited in a retirement account of diversified stocks and bonds—call it Plan B.

But before you choose that option, think for a moment about a world in which such compulsion does not exist, but everyone knows that they must provide for their own retirement if they want more than $10,000 a year. Today, many low-income people have never heard of diversification and long-term gains, because they have never had any money to invest and no need to plan for their own retirement. In the world of the Plan, talk about investments will be part of the morning conversations over coffee in small-town cafes and after work in blue-collar taverns. Part of that conversation will consist of wild-eyed schemes—but most of it will consist of the others ridiculing the dreamer, because the principle of diversification has become common knowledge. The option of using the law to require that investments from the grant be made in broad-based portfolios is open, but it is not really necessary. You won't have to be a genius or have connections on Wall Street to invest your retirement savings sensibly.

Of course there will be people who make decisions that you consider imprudent, but ask yourself why they should not be allowed to do so. Think of it this way: Over 40,000 people are killed every year in automobile accidents. The harm they suffer is not nearly as benign as having a lower retirement income than they could have enjoyed if they had behaved differently. They are dead. Close to three million people are injured every year in automobile accidents. Many of them are severely disabled for the rest of their lives, another penalty far more devastating than a loss of retirement income. And yet we permit anyone to drive who can pass a simple driving test that does nothing to measure the applicant's impulsiveness, drinking or drug habits, intelligence, or judgment—and, for that matter, does not even test his ability to drive except in the simplest conditions. A more thorough screening process to select qualified drivers is economically and technically feasible. By installing it, and consequently denying driving privileges to a substantial proportion of the American population, we could save thousands of lives per year. Given what is known about the relationship of the problematic driving traits to socioeconomic factors, we must expect the people who would be denied driving privileges to be disproportionately poor and disadvantaged.[15]

Do you favor such a policy? Those who do are at least being consistent when they oppose giving the mass of the population control over their own retirement funds. But if you do not think that 10 or 20 percent of the adult population should be denied the right to drive (and strict screening standards might disqualify even more), then you need to ask yourself why you are willing to countenance tens of thousands of deaths and millions of injuries per year in the name of the freedom to drive. Having answered that question for yourself, you should then ask why it is okay to tell people who are not clinically retarded or mentally ill that, for their own good and that of society as a whole, they should not be permitted to use the grant as they see fit.

Plan B is an option I could live with, but I hope to persuade you by the end of the book that it is inferior to a society in which people are free to make their own choices, including their own mistakes. The summary statement of the argument to come is this: Plan B will reduce the number of people who completely fritter away their retirement savings. But it will also reduce the ability of people to pursue their dreams for how to live their lives. Under a system where even the most foolish or the most unlucky will still have $10,000 a year until they die, and in a society that once again has a vital set of civic institutions to deal with misfortune, no one is going to starve in the streets. The greater freedom to do wonderful things with one's life is worth the greater freedom to make mistakes.

What about shorter time periods? The forty-five-year time period is the correct one to use if the question is whether twenty-one-year-olds should prefer the Plan or Social Security. But since many people defer their private saving for retirement until their thirties or later, it is important to note that the reliability of real returns remains high for shorter time periods. Consider, for example, the case of someone who waits until he is thirty-six to begin saving for retirement, giving him a thirty-year investment period. There were 171 overlapping thirty-year periods from 1802 to 2001. The worst of them still showed a profit, with a return of 2.7 percent. In 163 of those 171 periods—95 percent of them—the average annual return was more than 4 percent.

Even a person who has turned fifty-one and is looking at just a fifteen-year investment period should realize that out of the 186 such periods from 1802 to 2001, he would have lost money in just two of them (and then just barely), and would have averaged more than 4 percent in 148 of them (80 percent of the time).

What about the risks of trusting to the stock market versus the security of a government-backed guarantee? You have probably encountered an argument in the debate over proposals to privatize part of Social Security that goes something like this: "How can we rest the security of our elderly population on the vagaries of the stock market? No matter what the history of investments has been, we cannot be sure that the future will produce the same results. Better to maintain a system in which the government guarantees the result."[16]

In the specific case of the Plan, a guarantee of $10,000 a year remains. But the larger fallacy in that argument needs to be more widely recognized. *If stocks do not continue to appreciate in real value by an average of 4 percent over the next forty-five years, the government will not be able to make good on its promises anyway.* All of the government's promises depend on economic growth at least as robust as that implied by an anemic 4 percent average return in the stock market. If we institute the Plan and the next generation happens upon a forty-five-year period so catastrophic that their retirement fund goes bust, the current system will have gone bust as well. Here is the difference between the risks of the current system and the Plan: If you own your retirement account, you can make your own decisions about how to protect against the prospect of hard times. If your retirement remains with the government, you must trust politicians to foresee hard times and act wisely.

The main points to remember in thinking about the Plan and retirement are these:

- The Plan guarantees the universal income floor that the current system does not.

- The 4 percent assumption is conservative—and it produces a far larger retirement income than the current system, even for low-income workers.

- Trusting in the growth of the American economy is not a choice. The risks of the Plan are no greater than the risks of the current system.

4

Health Care

Under the Plan, people will be responsible for their own health care, as they were from the founding of the republic until 1965, except that every adult, including all those who do not have health insurance under the current system, will now have $10,000 to tap for dealing with their health-care needs. A pure version of the Plan will leave up to them whether to use that money foolishly or wisely, plan for the future or hope for the best.

But health care is *sui generis* in a variety of ways, so I will not leave the discussion at that. The current health-care system is peculiarly wrongheaded. Three reforms could transform it, and with those reforms the Plan would work much better. First, a few words about the nature of the problems posed by health care under the current system, and then the reforms.

The Inevitability of Choices

It has only been about seventy years since the quality of
health care began to make much difference to large numbers
of people.[1] Now health care can prolong life and improve
its quality in myriad ways. Everybody understandably wants
everything that contemporary medicine has to offer. Politicians around the world compete to promise voters that they
will get it, provided by the government, and people around
the world tend to vote for them.

The truth that politicians cannot admit is that no government can make good on the promise of universal state-
of-the-art health care, not even in a country as rich as the
United States. Medical advances have produced too many
possibilities to give everyone everything. In every country,
choices have to be made about who gets what care, based on
the same question that underlies every purchase: "Is it worth
it?" The issue is who makes that choice—an individual who
needs the care, or a government that doles it out.

The Falling Real Costs of Health Care

The health care story has a bright side, however, if only
we would stop to think about it: Except at its frontier,
health care should be getting cheaper. The real costs of the
routine things that keep you healthy and cure you of
most of the curable ailments have been going down. *Real
costs* means the actual dollar costs of medical equipment,

pharmaceuticals, facilities, and labor for accomplishing a given medical outcome.

The biggest reduction in costs has been produced by antibiotics, which have converted many formerly painful, expensive, and mortal ailments into minor problems. But the reduction in real costs has occurred in many things physicians do. Wounds that used to require stitching often can be closed with adhesives. Blood tests that used to require labor-intensive analysis are now done automatically by machines. Ulcers that used to require surgery are now controlled through inexpensive pills.

Cost-per-outcome has been dropping for many of the high-tech medical technologies. Laparoscopic surgery is an example: The cost of laparoscopic equipment is greater than the cost of a scalpel and retractors for traditional surgery, but the patient goes home sooner, saving hospitalization costs. Those savings occur with every operation, while the cost of the laparoscopic equipment is amortized over hundreds of operations.

Even the labor costs of health care should be falling. The potential reductions per outcome in labor costs are limited, because health care will always be more labor-intensive than most industries, but productivity per employee is rising nonetheless. Remote monitoring of symptoms means that fewer nurses can keep track of more patients. Improvements in technologies for everything from hospital beds to food preparation increase the productivity of support staff. If other forces weren't getting in the way, the cost of keeping a person in a hospital bed for a day would be going down.

The one way in which the real cost of health care naturally increases is through the expansion of the outcomes that medicine can achieve. They account for only a small proportion of the advances in medical science. The rest of the improvements involve better or more certain ways of achieving existing outcomes, and those are the ones for which costs should usually be stable or falling.

Choose and Pay

And yet the soaring cost of health care is one of the leading political issues of our day. How can this be? Because of the ways in which the laws governing health care ensure that costs rise. They are all variations on one theme: They shield the ultimate consumers of health care—you and me—from making the choice, "Is it worth it?" Three examples will illustrate.

Example #1: Routine medical problems. You trip on the basement stairs and end up with a two-inch gash in your arm that needs stitches and a tetanus booster. Now, you go to your private physician or the emergency room. The bill will reach three figures, paid by your employer-provided insurance. If you have no coverage and no cash, the cost of your visit to the ER will be passed on to the hospital's other patients—which is to say, passed on to insurance companies. If you are poor and on Medicaid, the cost will be passed on to government—which is to say, passed on to taxpayers.

Suppose the money were coming out of your own pocket. In that case, it might occur to you that you don't need to see a physician to get to the medical technician who will probably end up treating you anyway. The wholesale cost of the antiseptics, gauze, bandages, needle, surgical thread, Novocain, and tetanus booster comes to a few dollars. Add in the technician's salary and the overhead for a clinic, and getting that arm stitched up should cost only thirty or forty dollars, tops.

Legal barriers are the immediate reason such clinics are so rare, but why use one even if they are available—as long as you aren't paying for it?[2] Why go to a medical technician when you can see a physician? If, instead, patients had to look at a difference measured in hundreds of dollars out of their own pockets, the inexpensive clinic staffed by medical technicians would suddenly be attractive—and such medical clinics would spring up like McDonald's if given a chance to do so.

Example #2: Just-to-be-sure medicine. You turn sixty years old. You have high cholesterol and wonder whether you have clogged arteries. You visit a cardiologist, who gives you a stress test that reveals a few minor anomalies. He offers you the choice between a further test that would tell you a lot but leave some uncertainty, or a much more expensive procedure that gives a definitive answer. You choose the expensive one because, as long as the insurance company is paying for it, why not be sure? The bill is more than ten thousand dollars. You are happy to learn that your heart is in terrific shape. But there was nothing wrong to begin with.

If it had been a question of paying the bill yourself, you might have just gotten serious about your diet and exercise and not gone to see the cardiologist at all. If you had seen the cardiologist, you probably would have been satisfied with the less expensive diagnostic option.

Example #3. End-of-life care. Health care at the end of life—the phrase has become so much a term of art that it is often denoted by an acronym, EOL—involves the last few weeks or months when a disease is either terminal or so serious in a person of advanced age that the chances of recovery are negligible. As the ability of medical science to keep people alive has progressed, the costs of EOL care have soared. They presently account for about 11 percent of the total health-care budget and 27 percent of the Medicare budget—about $1,674 per Medicare enrollee per year as of 2002.[3] This is one of the least cost-effective ways of using limited government resources, and one of the least beneficial ways of using limited health-care resources.

Now imagine a world in which you are contemplating the purchase of alternative insurance policies for your old age. One policy will provide full coverage for EOL care, whatever it involves. The other provides for palliative and hospice care, but not hospitalization and curative therapies. The difference in the cost of the two policies over the course of years of payments will be thousands of dollars.

Perhaps you decide to choose the restricted policy, even though you are aware that you may have signed away a few months of earthly existence in exchange for more money

Sand Lake Town Library

In our hands, action to replace the welfare
state (Chad...

NOV 13 2018

10/16

Robert Fischer

Sand Lake Town Library

In our hands : a plan to replace the welfare
state / Charles Murray.

31182017092601

to spend now. You have made a voluntary choice about your own medical care as you approach death—but *you* have made it, not a government rationing system. Perhaps you pay the extra costs for unlimited EOL care. But *you* will be paying for it—the insurance rates will have been set to ensure that. The government is no longer in the position of requiring itself to pay tens of billions of dollars annually for EOL care.

Three Reforms for Approaching the Desired End-State

Taking care of your health-care needs should be like keeping your car on the road. You pay for the ordinary upkeep with cash and use insurance to protect against expensive accidents. The costs of gas and servicing that you pay as you go along are not cheap. Automobile insurance is not cheap. But even without a single government program to buy cars for poor people, these costs are so manageable that almost three-quarters of people below the official poverty line own a vehicle.[4]

Three reforms will go a long way toward enabling people to treat health care as they treat other expenses. None of them requires a large bureaucracy to administer it.

1. Legally obligate medical insurers to treat the entire population as a single pool.

2. Treat medical insurance provided as an employment benefit as taxable income.

3. Reform tort law so it becomes easy to write legally binding waivers and restrictions on liability.

I first discuss the reforms, then turn to the implications for the $10,000 cash grant.

Reform #1. Legally obligate medical insurers to treat the population, of all ages, as a single pool. This reform requires insurance companies to incorporate the population-wide incidence of all diseases across the age range into their insurance rates and to offer the same rate for the same package of coverage to everyone ages twenty-one and older, whether they are purchasing the policy as individuals or as part of a group.[5] The calculation that leads to these insurance rates should also include the high costs of care for chronic diseases.

A certain amount of unfairness is a cost of this reform. Its implementation could try to mitigate the unfairness by allowing insurance companies to charge smokers more than nonsmokers and hang-gliders more than people who do not hang-glide. But the line between personal choice and pre-existing conditions can be fuzzy (the case of obesity is an example). It may well turn out that the cost to the rest of us of subsidizing the health risks of obese smokers who hang-glide is only a few dollars per year per person, and the simplest solution for insurance companies and customers alike is to throw the personal-choice health risks into the one-pool pot along with other kinds of health risks. I will leave those calculations to the health-care specialists, observing simply that the requirement to treat the population as a single insurance pool is worth the residual unfairness if it eliminates the cosmic unfairness through which some people have genes or accidents that produce debilitation, pain, and physical handicaps that the rest of us are spared, through no fault or merit of anyone.

To make this work requires a tradeoff. Everyone, starting at age twenty-one, must use part of their grant to buy health insurance. This is one of the ways in which health care is *sui generis*: People at age twenty-one have radically different prospective needs for health care, and the information about those prospective needs is growing rapidly.[6] Even now that information is substantial. If one of your grandparents had multiple sclerosis and died at forty-five, your view about the importance of insurance in your twenties is going to be different from someone whose grandparents died at ninety-five. As genetic knowledge grows, so will our ability, and the ability of insurance companies, to know more about our future health problems.

Suppose the Plan leaves us free to decide whether to insure ourselves. It can be rational for someone in his twenties with a good family history to opt out of insurance for a while. This creates problems for others in their twenties who rationally want insurance because of a high-risk family history. If the set of people who buy health insurance is heavily weighted toward high-risk people in their twenties and thirties, plus people over forty, insurance premiums will be accordingly astronomical—and that is what would happen if the choice to buy insurance were voluntary. And so I stipulate that every American adult has to go into the insurance market starting at age twenty-one, buying a package that insures against medical catastrophe, whether the catastrophe consists of a single expensive operation or the cost of long-term care for chronic illnesses.[7]

The result is that the costs of comparatively unusual but extremely expensive health care needs are dispersed throughout the population, and young people with low health costs subsidize the cost of their care when they get old. Together, these considerations mean that insurance companies can offer an affordable premium throughout the lifespan.[8] To get a sense of what that premium would be under the current system, here are some numbers provided by a major insurance company:

If a normally healthy male about to turn twenty-one says, "I will irrevocably commit to a forty-five-year policy in return for a constant premium over those forty-five years," an insurance company under the current system could offer him comprehensive health insurance, plus pharmaceutical insurance, for about $2,800 annually, with a $2,500 deductible. For a woman in the same situation, the cost would be about $3,500.[9] Medicare disbursements per enrollee in 2002 were about $6,400.[10] If a person age twenty-one were to commit to a lifetime policy in a world without Medicare, the annual cost for comprehensive coverage until death would thus be somewhere in the $3,000 to $4,500 range (the cost would be so much lower than the per-person cost of Medicare for the same reason that a life insurance policy can be sold for a few dollars per thousand to a person in his twenties, even though the chance of an eventual claim for the entire amount is 100 percent). That figure is higher than the cost of a stripped-down package—it is based on the kind of comprehensive coverage that employer-funded plans typically provide, and on the cost structure of the current health-care system. Even so, the price is not astronomical, and it will get cheaper once reforms #2 and #3 are implemented as well.

I stipulated that the single-pool rule requires an insurance company to charge the same amount for a given package of coverage, whether the insured person is an individual or part of a group. This is important because of reform #2, to which I now turn.

Reform #2. Treat medical insurance provided as an employment benefit as taxable income. The single-pool rule will make individual medical insurance as cheap as the per-person cost of group insurance. Treating medical benefits as taxable income will lead millions of people to unlink their insurance from their jobs. This reform says to the employee: "Your medical benefit is worth X dollars, and you're going to pay income tax on that money. Would you rather have the cash instead?" If your company has provided precisely the coverage you want, you are indifferent—if you bought individual insurance, you would end up paying the same amount for the same coverage. But if you can get insurance that satisfies your needs for less money, you have an incentive to take the cash and provide for your own insurance.[11]

The first two reforms combined produce an insurance industry that sells a product to individuals who are looking for the right product for the lowest price—the crucial missing ingredient in the current market for health care.

Reform #3. Repeal medical licensing laws and alter tort law to make it made easy to write legally binding waivers and restrictions. Earlier, I said that low-cost medical clinics would proliferate like McDonald's franchises if they were given a chance. One of the things I had in mind by "given a chance" was the repeal of licensing laws that support a medical cartel.[12] But even if licensing laws are repealed, the second half of this reform is essential. Under today's tort jurisprudence, the neighborhood clinic I envisioned cannot have a piece of paper for you to sign when you walk in that says, in legally binding language, "We do minor medical repairs here. You can sue us if the arm we sew up becomes infected because we failed to sterilize our instruments, but not if you suffer a reaction from some exotic allergy." In the absence of such contracts, cheap medical care is impossible, because everything involving medical care is subject to strict legal scrutiny and large jury awards. Under the current system, it is as if you were not permitted to open a diner where your cook knows only how to cook hamburgers and fried eggs, but must hire a cook who can pass a master chef's exam. The costs this imposes on the system are enormous. As intellectually and technically demanding as some medical tasks are, a great many others are the profession's equivalent of cooking hamburgers and frying eggs.

This reform also addresses malpractice. The effects of jury awards for punitive damages are well publicized. In some especially vulnerable specialties, such as obstetrics,

EVOLVING STANDARDS

You wouldn't have to negotiate a contract every time you visited a health-care provider. Freedom to write binding contracts for medical services would quickly lead to some standard contracts that almost everybody would use. Their virtue is that they would be sensible. Most health-care providers don't want or expect to be freed from responsibility for incompetence. Most patients don't (before the fact) expect health-care providers to practice their craft with god-like perfection. A market for contracts will lead consumers and practitioners to converge on a few good ones that correspond with common sense and good faith.

Guarantees for new products provide an analogous case. Even without a law requiring it, almost all the products we buy are backed by guarantees that consumers find acceptable without having to negotiate them on a case-by-case basis. Successful health-care providers will figure out how to offer service agreements that meet the same demand of the market, and yet are ones that they can live with.

Why not have the government decide on reasonable standards? Because the government won't. It will be captive to the National Association of Trial Lawyers and the American Medical Association. If you want reasonable standards to evolve, let consumers who want affordable but competent health care come to their own agreements with health-care providers who seek their business.

malpractice insurance has become so expensive that large numbers of practitioners are leaving the field altogether. Malpractice awards add just as importantly to the bottom line for the consumer by inducing physicians to practice defensive medicine.[13] Many legislative solutions have been tried but with only modest success. The solution is to make waivers and restrictions easy and binding.

Affordable Health Care

The effects of these reforms will be to flatten the overall increases in health-care costs overall and drive down the cost of routine health care. This is not wishful thinking, but a straightforward consequence of changing the forces that currently affect the price of health care.

The first and inevitable effect is that millions of consumers will shift toward the desired end-state as I expressed it earlier: paying for regular health care out of pocket and insuring against catastrophe. More formally, people will shift to policies with high deductibles, or perhaps to no coverage at all for routine care. The shift will happen because the difference between the out-of-pocket costs of comprehensive coverage and restricted coverage will be large. The millions of people who have done that will become active consumers of inexpensive care for routine health problems, at the same time that the reform of tort law has permitted health-care providers to enter into limited-liability agreements with their customers. The market for, and then supply of, small, inexpensive clinics will expand, becoming a major part of the health-care system.

Putting numbers on the cost of health care under these circumstances is a matter of guesswork, but this much is sure: Costs will drop substantially. When health care is subjected to the same choices that people make about everything else in their lives—"Is it worth it to me?"—the health-care industry will respond in the same way as other industries constrained by market forces, with better products at lower cost.

For the rest of the book, I assume that $3,000 of the grant goes to health care from age twenty-one onward, an amount that in my best estimate would provide health care that meets any reasonable standard if the reforms have been installed, and basic health care if they have not. We need not be wedded to that precise figure, however. The sense of the proposition is this: Figure out the cost of a no-frills, high-deductible insurance policy that would pay for extraordinary health-care costs, including major surgery, all genetically based diseases, and illnesses involving long-term care. That is the amount of money that I am willing for the government to provide. If it is discovered that the number is $3,800, then I will be happy to make the grant $10,800. The arguments in the rest of the book assume $7,000 remains after health care is deducted. As long as this amount remains constant, the amount devoted to health care is irrelevant to those arguments. The main effect of tweaking the size of the grant would be to delay the crossover year when the Plan is no more costly than the current system.

5

Poverty

The topic of this chapter is poverty, meaning the lack of means to provide for basic material needs and comforts. I conceive of poverty along a dimension ranging from purely involuntary to purely voluntary. Involuntary poverty occurs when someone who plays by the rules is still poor. Poverty that I consider voluntary is the product of one's own idleness, fecklessness, or vice.

The immediate effect of the Plan is to end involuntary poverty. In a world where every adult starts with $10,000 a year, no one needs to go without decent food, shelter, or clothing. No one needs to do without most of the amenities of life, even when *amenities* is broadly defined. This statement holds even after taking the expenses of retirement and medical care into account. Here is the arithmetic, if we use the official poverty line as the definition for poverty:

We start with the rule stated at the end of the last chapter, assigning $3,000 to health care. Let's say that another

$2,000 is put toward retirement (voluntarily under the pure Plan, or through law under Plan B), invested annually in an index-based mutual fund. After paying for retirement and health care, the recipient has $5,000 left. What then must that person do to stay out of poverty?

The elderly need to do nothing. The official definition of poverty in 2002 meant an income of less than $8,628 for an unrelated individual age sixty-five or older, and $10,885 for a two-person household.[1] Assuming a $2,000 annual contribution and, as always, an average real return of 4 percent compounded annually, that person's retirement fund at age sixty-seven will stand at about $253,000, sufficient to purchase a lifetime annuity paying about $20,000 annually.[2] Adding in $7,000 from the continuing grant (no longer having to deduct $2,000 for retirement), the annual cash income of a single person upon retiring will be $27,000, or $54,000 for a couple. The grant plus annuity from the retirement savings puts an elderly individual living alone at more than three times the poverty line, and an elderly couple at about five times the poverty line.

A working-age individual living alone needs to work—but not very much, and not at a high-paying job. The official definition of poverty in 2002 meant an income of less than $9,359 for an unrelated individual under the age of sixty-five. Working forty-nine weeks and forty hours a week at the minimum wage of $5.15 an hour produces about $10,000. Combine that with the $5,000 not used for retirement and medical coverage, and the total income of $15,000 amounts to one-and-a-half times the poverty threshold. The economy is bad? Someone could be out of work for more than six months and still reach the poverty threshold by working at a minimum-wage job. For a couple without children, the poverty threshold in 2002 was $12,110. One person could be completely unemployed, and the other work just eleven weeks in a course of a year, and the couple would still be over the poverty line.

There are children to worry about? The poverty line for a couple with one child under 18 was $14,480 in 2002. If the mother stays home and the father works full time at a minimum wage job, the combined income of the parents after contributions to retirement and health care would be about $10,000 from the job plus $10,000 from the two grants, or a $20,000 family income, 38 percent higher than the poverty line. The economy is bad? The father can be unemployed for seven months out of the year and still reach the poverty line with a minimum-wage job, while the mother doesn't work at all.

I could extend the examples, but the point should be clear: Surpassing the official poverty line under the Plan is easy for people in a wide range of living circumstances, even in a bad economy, and even assuming jobs at the rock-bottom wage. To see how unrealistically stringent these conditions are, consider that the minimum wage I have been using is $5.15 an hour. The average janitor earns twice that—$10.28 an hour in 2002.[3] Under the Plan, the average janitor working forty hours a week for forty-eight weeks a year would have a total cash income of $24,738 plus money for health care and retirement.

Four objections may be raised: Using the official poverty line is too ungenerous a standard. I haven't considered the value of the present set of welfare programs available to low-income people that would be lost under the Plan. What about poor young adults under twenty-one who are not eligible for the grant? Who will care for those people who cannot work at all?

The official poverty line is too stingy. The official poverty line has only the fuzziest relation to actual poverty.[4] Let us assume for purposes of argument that it is too stingy, and substitute the definition of poverty adopted by European social democrats, an income of less than half the median income. Instead of taking the easy way out and using median income for the entire population, I will use median earnings of full-time, year-round workers as the basis. In 2002, that number was $35,590, half of which is $17,795.[5] To raise the bar still higher, let's not count the $5,000 set aside for retirement and medical care as part of income. This demanding definition of "being out of poverty" can still be reached with a minimum-wage job. It would mean forty-eight hours a week for fifty-two weeks a year—a lot of hours, but fewer than large numbers of Americans, including many readers of this book, routinely work without feeling overburdened. If the average janitor is the person in question, he would reach half the median income with just thirty-one forty-hour weeks of work. The Plan enables people to escape poverty under poverty's most liberal definition.

I haven't considered the value of the canceled programs.
Under the Plan, many programs to help the poor would be
gone: the earned income tax credit (EITC), temporary assistance for needy families (TANF, the cash payment that used
to be called AFDC), food stamps, Medicaid, housing subsidies, and the other programs listed in appendix A. In net,
which poor people would benefit under the Plan? Who
would lose more than they gain?

All low-income married or cohabiting couples in which
at least one person works for a substantial portion of the
year are better off under the Plan everywhere, children or
no children. Consider the highest-benefit state in the conti-
nental United States, California (Alaska is the highest of all
fifty states, for exceptional reasons), and a couple with one
child in which the man earns just $10,000 and the woman
doesn't work at all. Under the current system, the family
gets about $2,662 in EITC, $1,000 from TANF, and $3,900
in food stamps—a total of $7,562 in cash or cash-like bene-
fits, plus a package of other in-kind benefits.[6] The Plan gives
that same couple a package worth $20,000—not a close
comparison, even in California.

If neither the man nor the woman works at all—an
extreme case indeed—the Plan is better for couples everywhere except the highest-benefit states, and even there it is a
close call. In 2002, a California couple with a child in which
neither partner worked at all got about $8,100 in cash from
TANF and $4,700 from food stamps, plus other in-kind ben-
efits. The total value of those benefits might exceed $20,000,
depending on how the in-kind benefits are valued, but not

by much. In less generous states, even couples who don't work at all are better off under the Plan.

Virtually all single, low-income males would benefit. Under the current system, their main benefit is the EITC. But the maximum value of the EITC is only about $4,000. Add in the maximum food stamp allowance a man might get, and males are better off under almost every scenario. The exception is a single man with no income who has custody of children and who lives in a high-benefit state, but that constitutes a minuscule proportion of poor males.

The one major category of people who would get the grant but who are better off financially under the current system is single mothers who have no earnings or low earnings. Everywhere in the country, even in the low-benefit states, a case can be made that the total value of their benefits package is greater than $10,000. Theoretically, the Plan does not become clearly preferable for such women until earnings exceed $13,000 to $18,000, depending on the number of children and the state. I say "theoretically" because, under the current system, many women who qualify for benefits of this magnitude do not actually get them (many who legally qualify do not apply). In contrast, all single mothers will get the full $10,000 under the Plan.

I should also note that single mothers under the Plan do not need to live in poverty. First, they have the choice to work. If they work most of the year at a minimum-wage job, their earnings plus the grant get them out of poverty. In addition, a woman living under the Plan can get child support that is often unavailable under the current system—the father of her child has a monthly income arriving at a known bank account that can be tapped, and modern DNA analysis makes identification of the biological father easy (see chapter 6 for more on this).

But the greater availability of child support is only one of many new possibilities a single mother has for coping with her situation under the Plan. Even if a woman decides not to work but has $7,000 in cash to bring to the table (or $5,000 under Plan B), she can find some joint living arrangement with family or friends, or find some other group with whom to pool her resources. A single mother living in a world where she has the grant, and so do her family and friends, has a variety of ways to avoid poverty—by her own choices and actions, not by the dispensation of a bureaucracy.

What about poor young adults under twenty-one who are not eligible for the grant? Who will care for those people who cannot work at all? I group these two questions because the answer to both is the same, and it extends the point I just made about single mothers over twenty-one: The key to understanding the effects of the Plan is not that it provides each individual adult with $10,000 per year, but that it provides *all* adults with $10,000 per year. "In our hands" refers not only, nor even primarily, to "our hands" as individuals, but "our hands" as families, communities, and civil society as a whole. I discuss those who cannot work at all because of physical or mental incapacity in chapter 11. I discuss people under the age of twenty-one in chapter 6. The bottom line is this: Under the Plan, hardly anyone will

What Should Be Expected of People Who Have Had Tough Breaks?

Whether the paragraphs above are self-evidently true or unrealistically optimistic depends on one's premises about what human beings can be expected to do. Many observers on the left (and some on the right) argue that millions of people cannot be expected to go out and work at minimum-wage jobs or otherwise cope with daily life because of disadvantages they have suffered— racism, broken homes, poor education, poverty, and the like. I have just asserted that the number of people who cannot be expected to meet those standards is small.

I work from the premise that everyone not clinically retarded or mentally ill makes choices. Some people are able to make only the most basic choices, but one of those basic choices is whether to seek work and take it when offered. Another basic choice open to everyone is whether to behave cooperatively with family and neighbors. Conversely, failure to seek work or failure to behave cooperatively are choices. To deny that these are choices is to deny the humanity of the people we want to help.

be forced to live in poverty, compared to the 11–14 percent of the population that has been classified as poor in the United States for the last thirty years.

The fact that no able-bodied person *needs* to live in poverty doesn't mean that no one *will* live in poverty. Some people behave in ways that ensure they will live in squalor, will not have enough money to buy food, or will be evicted for not paying the rent. They may drink away their money or gamble it away. Some people will be feckless under any system. The Plan ends involuntary poverty—the kind that exists when people have done the ordinary things right and are still poor. These are the people who most deserve help. Under the Plan, their poverty is ended.

6

The Underclass

The underclass denotes a class of people who exist at the margins of American society. They are usually poor, but poverty is a less important indicator than personal behavior destructive to themselves and to their communities. Membership in the underclass is not a yes/no proposition, but three categories of people constitute a large part of the problem: chronic criminals, never-married women with children, and able-bodied young men who are out of the labor force.[1] How might the Plan affect them?

Criminality

According to sociological theory that sees crime as a response to economic deprivation, the Plan should reduce crime. The Plan will provide a nice test of such theories. But the twentieth century provided a nice test, too, and the theories flunked. Poverty fell; crime rose.[2] The Plan may indirectly reduce crime through positive effects on family structure, but I will not forecast reduced crime as one of the Plan's positive effects. If it happens, it will be a bonus.

Births to Single Women

The effects of the Plan on children are likely to be a large net positive, reducing births to single women and increasing births to married women, thereby markedly reducing the proportion of births that occur to single women. Consider three categories of women: single women under twenty-one, single women twenty-one and older, and married women of all ages.

Single women under twenty-one. The Plan radically increases the economic penalty of having a baby for a single woman under twenty-one, an age group that accounts for about a third of all births to single women.[3] She no longer gets any government assistance—no cash payment, no food stamps, no Medicaid, no housing subsidies, no subsidies for day care.[4]

The Plan also increases the economic penalty on the parents of a teenage mother who is still living at home. At present, the net financial effect on her parents is offset by the stream of benefits that accompanies the baby. Under the Plan, the costs of the new baby will fall on the girl's parents (in low-income neighborhoods, typically just her mother). The incentives to pressure the daughter to avoid pregnancy will increase.

The Plan increases the likelihood that the father of the child faces an economic penalty. In today's low-income neighborhoods, having sex with many women confers social status on the male.[5] When a child results, many fathers pay nothing; others give minor support for a few years and then fade away.[6] Many states have passed legislation to make unmarried fathers pay child support, but such efforts confront a problem: many of these fathers have no visible income, and enforcing child-support orders is difficult even when they do. Under the Plan, every man age twenty-one or older has $583 deposited to a known bank account every month (in this and other calculations henceforth, I assume that $3,000 of the grant is allocated to health care and that retirement contributions are not mandatory). Police do not need to track him down or try to find him on a day when he has cash on hand. All they need is a court order to tap the bank account. Even teenage fathers who are not yet getting the grant need not escape. Just write the child-support law so that their obligation accumulates until they turn twenty-one. The state pays the child support until then, at which time his cash grant is tapped not only for the continuing child support but to pay back the money already spent.

In other words, every party to the birth of a child to a single woman under the age of twenty-one suffers immediate and large increased costs under the Plan. Many young women will take steps to avoid getting pregnant that they do not take now. Among those young women who do get pregnant, larger proportions will choose to give the baby up for adoption or to have an abortion.[7] The net effect will be a large reduction in the number of babies born to and raised by single teenage girls.

Single women twenty-one and older. Every unmarried woman over the age of twenty-one will have $7,000 to pay for the costs of a baby. This is somewhat less than the value of the package of benefits in an average state that a single mother gets now, but the reduced amount of benefits is not the main consideration.[8] The big difference is that, under the current system, the birth of a baby brings resources that would not be offered if the baby did not exist. Under the Plan, the baby will be a drain on resources. Consider the implications of this difference for three categories of women: (1) women who want to have babies, (2) women who don't want to have babies and who value having income to spend on themselves, and (3) women who want to have babies, but also value income to spend on themselves.

In many states, women in category 1 will get less under the Plan than under the current system and thereby will have some increased incentive to avoid pregnancy. But $7,000 is enough to enable them to do what they want to do anyway—have a baby—so I do not predict major changes in their fertility.

Everyone in category 2 has a substantial incentive to avoid getting pregnant under the Plan. Under the current system, a woman who does not want to get pregnant is at least compensated if she has a baby. Under the Plan, having a baby is pure economic loss.

Women in category 3 think that the prospect of having a baby is attractive, but so is having money to spend on themselves. The less eager a woman is to have a baby, the greater the likelihood that under the Plan she will avoid getting pregnant. But every woman in category 3 faces a major change: Under the current system, she is subsidized for doing something she wanted to do anyway. Under the Plan, she will have to bear a cost for doing the same thing.

I have framed the argument in the abstract, but it will not be abstract when the Plan goes into effect. Think in terms of a twenty-year-old woman from a low-income neighborhood with a boyfriend. She knows she is about to start receiving a monthly check of $583 a month. She also knows women in her neighborhood who are already getting that check. The ones without babies are spending it on themselves. Her friends with babies are buying diapers and baby food, and probably living with their mothers because they cannot afford a place of their own. Under the Plan, the opportunity costs of having a baby will be obvious and alarming to low-income young women in the same way that they have always been obvious and alarming to middle-class and affluent young women.

Married women in low-income communities. Almost all young married couples want to have children eventually. Some of those couples defer having a child or limit the number of children for economic reasons. The low-income portion of that group will have up to $14,000 in additional family income under the Plan, making a first child or an additional child financially more feasible. There is no counterbalancing group for which the Plan makes having children less attractive. It seems to be a sure bet that births to low-income and working-class married couples will go up.[9] The reason this is important to the underclass is that it increases the availability of role models for young men in poor neighborhoods. It is possible to grow up in some inner-city neighborhoods without ever knowing a man who acts as a good father to his children and a good husband to his wife. Increasing the number of such visible men is arguably as important as reducing the number of births to single women.[10]

Young Males Not in the Labor Market

The third category of people who embody the underclass consists of able-bodied young men in low-income neighborhoods who do not work or even look for work. Through the middle of the twentieth century, such young males were rare. Since the middle of the 1960s, they have become common, especially among young black males.[11] I will take 1999 as the example, at the height of the economic boom of the 1990s, when jobs were available everywhere in the country even for people with no job experience and no skills. Of males ages sixteen to twenty-four who were not enrolled in school, 8 percent of whites and 22 percent of blacks were not working and not looking for work.[12]

Some of these men live with parents. Some live with girlfriends. Many have income, but not from regular jobs. The money may come from crime, the gray market, or sporadic day-work. How will the Plan affect their behavior after they reach their twenty-first birthdays?

One possibility is that the Plan's work disincentives will increase the number of young men and young women who leave the labor market. That worry is not restricted to the underclass but to everyone, and requires a chapter of its own (the next one). For now, I am talking exclusively about young men over twenty-one who already have dropped out of the labor market even without the Plan.

The Plan complicates their lives. It forces them to have an income, and one that other people know about. That fact produces a cascading set of consequences through what I call the Doolittle Effect, for reasons explained in the box on the next page.

Consider first the young men who have persuaded parents or girlfriends to provide them with a place to live and food. The Plan goes into effect. Suddenly it is known to both parents and girlfriends that their lodger has $583 being deposited into a bank account in his name every month. For most parents and girlfriends, the situation will now have changed materially.

Some of these young men will be kicked out. They were allowed to live in the house or apartment on sufferance because they claimed to have no other options. Now they undeniably have options. Other men will find that the parent or girlfriend now insists on receiving a portion of the $583. The man faces a monetary price for his lifestyle that did not previously exist.

Furthermore, that price is constantly subject to an increase: When the sponsoring parent or girlfriend runs into

GEORGE BERNARD SHAW'S VERSION OF THE PLAN

In *Pygmalion* and later in *My Fair Lady*, Alfred P. Doolittle is an able-bodied man often out of the labor force who fathered Eliza without marrying her mother. Then Henry Higgins recommends him as the most original moralist in England and Alfred is consequently willed a large income by an American businessman. Here is the *Pygmalion* version of Alfred's lament about his changed situation:

> I touched pretty nigh everybody for money when I wanted it. . . . Now I'm worried; tied neck and heels; and everybody touches me for money. . . . A year ago I hadn't a relative in the world except two or three who wouldn't speak to me. Now I've fifty, and not a decent week's wages among the lot of them. I have to live for others now, not for myself: that's middle-class morality.

It is suggested he could just give back the money if that's the way he feels about it. Alfred replies, "That's the tragedy of it. . . . It's easy to say chuck it, but I haven't the nerve."[13]

Thus the Doolittle Effect.

a financial shortfall, he will be asked to help out. Before, the young man had a claim on their support. Now, the parent or girlfriend has a claim on the young man.

The incentives for this young man to get a job will also have changed. Let's say that he could get a low-wage job netting him $1,000 a month. Under the current system, he would be pressured to spend a large part of that $1,000 on the housing and food that he had been getting for nothing. If he moved out, almost all of the $1,000 in earned income would be eaten up by those costs. A full-time job would provide only a few hundred dollars' difference in discretionary income. Moving out and working is unattractive. He stays put—rationally, in the short term.

The Plan gives him an income stream whether he wants it or not. Large numbers of these young men will find themselves forced to pay for rent and food. The only choice open to a man who finds himself under that pressure is to pay the girlfriend or parent or find his own place and buy his own food. Some men like living with the parents or girlfriend, and do not move. But for those who, *ceteris paribus*, prefer a place of their own, taking a job now makes economic sense. To take a simple example, suppose that the man finds himself having to pay exactly $583 per month for food and rent to a girlfriend. Under the Plan, a $1,000-per-month job provides him with $1,000 in additional discretionary income. It will not often be that simple in practice, but the principle generalizes: A man who has been living off others and then acquires an income stream will typically find that it has become rational to move out if he works. He has gone from a situation in which he had little incentive to work to a situation in which he has substantial incentive to work.

It is hard to say whether the Doolittle Effect will include pressure to marry the mother of his child. In an age when cohabitation has become common, perhaps not, especially in states where child support can be enforced as easily against men who have never married the mother as against those who did. But pressures to act like a father will probably increase. A man with a steady income, as every man will have under the Plan, is treated differently from a man without a steady income. The fact of his income gives him a standing in others' calculations, including the assumption that a man can be pushed to shoulder responsibilities.

I have no empirical basis for forecasting the proportions of idle young men who would fall in the various categories I have described. Some will doubtlessly use the grant as a way of continuing to be idle. But for others the Doolittle Effect will be real.

These chapters are about immediate changes in tangible incentives, not about the longer-range effects. But I cannot leave the discussion of effects on the underclass without alluding to a broader effect of the Plan that may be the most important of all.

A persuasive critique of the current system is that the people who make up the underclass have no reason to think they can be anything else. They are poorly educated, without job skills, and living in neighborhoods where prospects are bleak. The quest for dignity and self-respect takes the form of trying to beat the system, whether *the system* means the criminal code or the rules that surround the distribution of welfare. The more fortunate members of society may see such people as obstinately refusing to take advantage of the opportunities that exist. Seen from the perspective of the man who has never held a job or the woman who wants to have an infant to love, those opportunities look fraudulent.

The Plan does not exhort the young man to go out and get a job. It does not urge the young woman to delay child-bearing. It does not do anything that tries to stage-manage their lives. The Plan provides a stake—prospectively for those under twenty-one, in actuality for those who have turned twenty-one. The grant is not charity—everyone in the country turning twenty-one is getting the same thing. Seven thousand dollars of it consists of cash to be used as they wish, not little bundles of benefits to be allocated as the welfare bureaucracy sees fit. The grant is deposited monthly into that most middle-class of institutions, a bank account. The Plan says just one thing to people who have never had reason to believe it before: "Your future is in your hands." And it is the truth.

7

Work Disincentives

The most serious practical objection to the Plan is its potential effect on work. For years, economists have found through rigorous quantitative analysis what common sense predicts: Make it easier not to work, and people work less. Unemployment insurance is the most obvious example, but almost any transfer payment linked to employment or wages has a similar effect, known to economists as a work disincentive.

Two specific groups subject to work disincentives under the Plan are discussed elsewhere: Young men who are out of the labor force under the current system (chapter 6) and women who now work but would quit to become full-time housewives (chapter 10). In the former case, there is no downside to the Plan (this group is already out of the labor force) and some upside (the Doolittle Effect). In the latter case, I argue that the reduction in work outside the home represents a positive net effect, not a negative one. This chapter restricts itself to the people who might stop working because of the cash grant, not to pursue some other equally productive life course, but to loaf.

The Plan does not even require such people to be sneaky. It says to twenty-one-year-olds, "If half a dozen of you want to pool your grants, rent a cottage on an inexpensive beach, and surf for the rest of your lives, the American taxpayer will support you." The question is how many people are likely to respond to the grant in that way or, more broadly, how labor force participation and work effort might be expected to change.

The following discussion works through a variety of scenarios, but here is where it will come out:

- Most of those who remain out of the labor force will be the same people who are out of the labor force under the current system.

- Most of the reductions in work effort will involve fewer hours worked, not fewer people working.

- Most of the people who leave the labor force will be college graduates who take time off between graduation and a permanent job or graduate school.

- The net decrease in work effort will be acceptable.

The key features of the Plan that lead to these conclusions are two buffer zones: the income level at which the grant begins to be paid back through the surtax, and the age at which the grant begins. By the time people have crossed these buffer zones, most of them will have passed the point at which living off the grant is an acceptable alternative.

The High Payback Point

To put it baldly, the rules of the Plan lure people into working until they are making so much money that they cannot
afford to quit.

To understand the problem that the rules are designed to
solve, consider the experience of the 1970s, when the United
States government conducted the negative income tax experiment in a few test cities (see chapter 1). The evaluators found
that large numbers of low-income young people dropped out
of the labor force. The reason was simple: When the government puts a floor on income, people in jobs that pay less than
the floor are effectively working for nothing.

The work disincentive does not stop there. Even a person making more than the floor can be working for pennies
an hour. If the floor is $200 a week, for example, and the job
offer is $250 for a forty-hour week, taking the job means
working for $1.25 an hour. For practical purposes, the
choices for people near the NIT's income floor were to take
the NIT and not work, work off the books and get the NIT
illegally, or work on the books and be a chump. Not sur-
prisingly, many people decided not to choose the last option.

Policy planners for the negative income tax experiment
tinkered with the incentives so that a dollar of income did
not produce a full dollar's reduction in the subsidy, but they
were up against mathematical constraints. There is no way to
set a simple floor under income anywhere near the poverty
line that does not have disastrous consequences for work
effort among people just getting into the labor market.

Setting the start of the payback of the grant at $25,000 is an Alexandrian solution, cutting the knot rather than trying to untie it. "Keep every cent you make until you reach $25,000, then we'll talk," it says. By that time, it is too late to back out. If someone is earning $25,000 a year under the Plan, still getting the full grant, he is taking home a cash gross of $32,000.[1] The 20 percent surtax on incremental income when he gets a raise to, say, $26,000 amounts to $200, leaving him with a cash gross of $32,800, compared to $7,000 if he stops working. The fact that someone starts paying a few hundred dollars in surtax when he first gets past $25,000 in earned income has no meaningful effect on his calculations about whether to continue working.[2]

For someone making $40,000 per year, the tax on the grant has risen to $3,000. By that point there will be significant effects on wage structure and on work effort at the margin (for hourly workers, interest in working overtime will drop off, for example). But the number of people making $40,000 who will decide to leave a $44,000 lifestyle (the sum of wages and the $4,000 in cash from the grant) for a $7,000 lifestyle will be small.[3] The work effect will be concentrated in hours, not jobs.

The Age at Which the Grant Begins

The second buffer zone is established by the three-year gap between the end of high school and the beginning of the grant. During that time, young people either have to earn their own living or continue to be supported by their parents. Consider how this buffer zone applies to specific groups of young people turning twenty-one and newly eligible for the grant.

Young people who go to work after high school. More than a third of all young people ages eighteen to twenty are neither in high school nor in college.[4] Under the Plan, they are not yet getting the grant, and getting a job after high school will make as much sense under the Plan as it does now.

Those who go to work will typically change jobs several times during the three years from eighteen to twenty-one, usually to take a better job requiring more skills for more money. By age twenty-one, the typical high school graduate working full time makes about $20,000 a year.[5] For that typical young worker looking at the first grant check, the choice is to continue working and live on $27,000 a year, or stop working and live on $7,000 a year. The high school graduate who has been working has already reached the point where quitting usually carries an unacceptably high price tag. The same calculus applies generally. Suppose that a less-fortunate twenty-one-year-old is still making only $10,000. Under the Plan, he could quit and have the same income. But another way of looking at it, and a potent one for any twenty-one-year-old who has unsatisfied consumer desires, is that he is about to get a $7,000 raise plus medical expenses if he keeps doing what he is already doing.

These financial calculations are independent of another effect of the buffer zone: By the time they are twenty-one, many high school graduates are not working just because of the money. They have acquired the habit of employment, are in skilled jobs that have good prospects, and are enjoying their work.

Young people who go to college. By the time they reach twenty-one, those who are still in college are usually about three-quarters of the way through an undergraduate degree. The onset of the grant is irrelevant to their long-term plans. Most have career ambitions. All expect to get jobs paying a decent wage, and many of them reasonably expect to be making more than $50,000 within a few years of graduation. The only effect is short term, giving students from less-affluent families more of the options that are already enjoyed by large numbers of college students from affluent families—travel abroad and unpaid internships being the most common choices. I assume that the Plan will have this effect, encouraging a significant number of college students to take some time off either during college or after graduation. Should this effect of the Plan be considered bad or good? Good, in my view (I have encouraged my own children to delay graduate school or career until after graduation). But I will not insist on this interpretation. An uncontroversial conclusion is that a few years off for this group will, at worst, do no great harm.

How many students will be permanently seduced into living in a beach house with their buddies, surfing their lives away? I could work through the pressures on them, social and economic, not to do so, but doing so seems like overkill. I find no reason to think that the number is going to be

GOING TO COLLEGE: THE PLAN VERSUS THE CURRENT SYSTEM FOR LOW-INCOME STUDENTS

Among the programs axed under the Plan are all government-paid student loans and scholarships. In their place, the Plan gives every young person cash. The amount of cash compares favorably with the federal scholarship program. As of 2005, federal "Pell Grants" top out at $4,050 per year. The Plan compares favorably with student loans insofar as no repayment is required. But the grant does not begin until the twenty-first birth-day. The Plan forces some students from low-income families to wait.

It is not clear how many would have to wait. Under the Plan, low-income students could use the guarantee of the grant as collateral to take to banks and to college financial offices. It is also plausible to expect a shift in the funding priority that foundations give to scholarships for low-income students when the federal government is no longer in that business. But I nonetheless stipulate that some low-income students who now go directly to col-lege after high school will, under the Plan, have to wait until they are twenty-one. Is this good or a bad? As in the case of taking time off after college, parents will differ in their opinions for reasons that are hard to evaluate empir-ically (I am in favor of waiting[6]). Ask someone who teaches in a public university where many students enter after some years working or serving in the military, and I pre-dict you will hear that the seriousness with which these students approach their education contrasts favorably

(continued on next page)

(continued from previous page)

> with that of the students who come to college directly from high school. But once again I do not insist on my interpretation. Under the Plan, every young person—*every* young person, not just those who obtain scholarships and grants under the current system—will have the financial wherewithal to further their education. They just won't have it until age twenty-one.

larger than the number of college graduates in the 1960s who became permanent hippies. Playing is fun for a while, but it gets old quickly.

If the Plan were to be implemented, it is prudent to assume that some decrease in work effort would occur. But the two buffer zones offer protections against work disincentives that none of the previous plans for a negative income tax have incorporated. If the Plan were to become a live political possibility, then the arguments I have presented should be subjected to econometric modeling, and the range of likely outcomes should be calibrated as accurately as possible. But we are now at a much earlier stage, where the question is whether unacceptable work disincentives should keep us from considering the Plan any further. The answer to that question seems to me plainly to be no.

PART III

The Larger Purpose

8

The Pursuit of Happiness in Advanced Societies

Put aside the immediate effects of the Plan as I have described them and consider instead this completely different proposition: The real problem advanced societies face has nothing to do with poverty, retirement, health care, or the underclass. The real problem is how to live meaningful lives in an age of plenty and security.

Throughout history, much of the meaning of life was linked to the challenge of staying alive. Staying alive required being a contributing part of a community. Staying alive required forming a family and having children to care for you in your old age. The knowledge that sudden death could happen any time required attention to spiritual issues.

Life in an age of plenty and security requires none of those things. Being part of a community is not necessary. Marriage is not necessary. Children are not necessary. Attention to spiritual issues is not necessary. It is not only possible but easy to go through life with a few friends and serial sex partners, earning a good living, having a good time, and dying in old age with no reason to think that one has done anything more significant than while away the time.

Perhaps, as the song says, that's all there is. But if you disagree, and think that to live a human life has—or *can* have—transcendental meaning, join me on an exploration that will take us far afield from annuity values and insurance pools, but will ultimately, I believe, point to the momentous effect of the Plan: the revitalization of the institutions through which people live satisfying lives.

This chapter lays out a framework for those statements. First, I use Western Europe as an advanced example of a problem that is beginning to confront the United States. Then I offer some propositions about the raw materials for living a happy life. I conclude with some propositions about the nature of man as a political and social animal and how they relate to the Plan.

Western Europe as the Canary in the Coal Mine

"An age of plenty and security" refers most accurately to Western Europe. Western Europe adopted the welfare state earlier than the United States and implemented it more completely. It was implemented earliest and most sweepingly in Germany, France, the Low Countries, and Scandinavia. Putting aside for a moment the budgetary crisis looming for these countries in the years ahead, they succeeded in their central goals. On almost any dimension of material well-being, these countries lead the world. Their indices of economic equality are the highest, and their indices of economic deprivation are the lowest. In the minds of many, the European welfare state represents the ideal America should emulate.[1]

It is an ideal only for a particular way of looking at life. It accepts that the purpose of life is to while away the time as pleasantly as possible, and the purpose of government to enable people to do so with as little effort as possible—what I will call the Europe Syndrome.

Europe's short work-weeks and frequent vacations are one symptom of the Syndrome. The idea of work as a means to self-fulfillment has faded. The view of work as a necessary evil, interfering with the higher good of leisure, dominates. The Europe Syndrome also consists of ways in which vocation is impeded. Job security is high, but so is the danger that if you leave a job to seek a better one, you won't be able to find one. Starting a new business is agonizingly difficult. Elaborate restrictions impede employers from rewarding merit and firing the incompetent. The Europe Syndrome is dismissive of all the ways in which work can become vocation and vocation can become a central source of satisfaction in life.

The precipitous decline of marriage is another symptom. As fast as the marriage rate has dropped in the United States, by about a quarter since 1970, it is still 50–90 percent higher (depending on the country) than in the advanced welfare states of Western Europe.[2] Part of the reason is direct: The advanced welfare state removes many of the traditional economic incentives to marry. But the larger reason involves the welfare state's effect on another reason for marriage: the desire to have children as a couple. The welfare state treats children as a burden to their parents that must be lightened through child allowances, subsidies, and services. The people of Europe have responded by agreeing. Children are no longer the central expression of a marriage and a life, but are objectified. Which to do, have a baby or buy a vacation home? Such is the calculus that young European adults routinely express when asked about their plans for children, and the value of the vacation home looms large. Why have a child, when children are so expensive, so much trouble—and, after all, what good are they, really? Such are the attitudes that young European adults routinely express when asked why they have no children. And so, throughout Europe, fertility rates have fallen far below replacement level.[3] This historically unprecedented phenomenon signifies more than a demographic trend. It reflects a culture of self-absorption—absorption not in some great ambition, but in the whiling away of life as pleasantly as possible.

The secularization of Europe is another symptom of the Europe Syndrome. Churches are empty. Europeans have broadly come to believe that humans are a collection of activated chemicals that, after a period of time, deactivate— nothing more. The causal arrow linking the welfare state and secularization could operate in either of two ways. If one believes there is no God and no transcendent meaning to life, then one might see the disappearance of religion in Europe as a valid consequence of the economic security that the welfare state has fostered. Religion was a way to cope with anxiety and misery. Take away the anxiety and misery, and religion falls away, too. Conversely, one may start by believing that God exists and life has transcendent meaning, but that the welfare state distracts humans from thinking about such things. Give people plenty and security, and they will fall into spiritual torpor. Whichever logic one employs, this unique secularization—no culture in recorded history has been nearly as secular as contemporary Europe's—cannot be blamed simply on modernity and economic wealth. Religion is alive and well in the United States. Secularization has occurred specifically in the advanced welfare states.

The same absorption in whiling away life as pleasantly as possible explains why Western Europe has become a continent with neither dreams of greatness nor the means to reacquire greatness. Europe's former scientific preeminence has vanished, as young scientists flock to American universities and corporations, even when they would prefer to live in their homelands, because they cannot hope for the professional freedom or financial support to pursue their work until they have crept up the bureaucratic chain. Even Europe's popular culture is largely borrowed from America, and its high culture can draw only on its glorious past—it has no contemporary high culture worthy of the name. All of Europe combined has neither the military force nor the political will to defend itself. The only thing Europe has left is economic size, and even that is growing at a slower pace than elsewhere. When life becomes an extended picnic, with nothing of importance to do, ideas of greatness become an irritant.

Such is the nature of the Europe Syndrome. The next issue is whether it is so awful. What's wrong with a society in which everyone one can while away life as pleasantly as possible? The answer requires an inquiry into the difference between pleasure and happiness.

Happiness Taken Seriously

A familiar word used in its original meaning can sometimes provoke fresh thinking. *Happiness* is one of those words. Social scientists may talk about quality of life and utility functions and cost-effectiveness, but the ultimate measure of the success of a policy is that it enables people to pursue happiness in the sense that Jefferson used *happiness* in the Declaration of Independence. His understanding drew from a tradition going back to Aristotle, but its gist can be stated quickly and simply: *Happiness is lasting and justified satisfaction with one's life as a whole.* If that is indeed the nature of happiness, it cannot be synonymous with pleasure. Consider the key words in that definition, *lasting* and *justified*.

Lasting says that when you think about how happy you are, you don't base it on momentary gratification. A bowl of hot buttered popcorn provides a satisfaction of a sort, as does a good movie, but they are not lasting satisfactions. The constraint of *lasting* limits the qualifying satisfactions to a narrow set.

Justified implies that satisfactions are not equally valid. Specifically, *justified* draws from an idea about happiness that the ancients and the Founders alike took for granted:

Happiness is inextricably linked with the exercise of one's abilities and the practice of virtue. Happiness consists of something more than feeling good. A pig cannot be happy. A person permanently high on drugs cannot be happy. An idle person cannot be happy. A selfish or cruel person cannot be happy. None meet the *justified* criterion.

Some Propositions about the Raw Materials for Happiness

If you consider yourself happy, ask yourself about the sources of your happiness. To the extent that you are not happy, what is lacking? I will suggest some answers, and you may judge how closely they fit your own.

Think of the pursuit of happiness as a process that each of us conducts by employing five raw materials. Two of these raw materials are passive: enough material resources and enough safety. This is as simple as saying that you cannot be happy if you are starving or constantly in danger.[4] I call them *passive* raw materials because possessing enough material resources and safety does not in itself make us happy, but their absence can keep us from being happy. Public policy directly affects the passive ingredients for the pursuit of happiness. Providing enough safety is the function of the police, the courts, and the armed forces. Providing enough material resources was historically the indirect effect of a government's sound economic policy and, more recently, has been adopted as the job of the welfare state.

I propose that the three active raw materials for the pursuit of happiness—those things which themselves can engender a sense of happiness—are intimate relationships with other human beings, vocation, and self-respect. A few words about each:

Intimate relationships with other human beings are achieved most commonly through a spouse and children, but they can also occur with friends, mentors, protégés, or colleagues. Conversely, unhappiness commonly results from the absence of satisfying, deep personal relationships.

Vocation might mean a job, or it might mean some other activity that engages one's passion. The chief characteristic of vocation as I am using the word is that it represents something a person is good at, his way of expressing his skills, of achieving his potential. Conversely, lack of happiness is likely to have something to do with a sense that one has never found such an outlet—that one has no vocation. *Vocation* as I am using the word could also be defined as self-fulfillment.

Self-respect is to some degree a necessary condition for happiness. It is hard to imagine a person being happy who does not have self-respect. But it can also serve as a substitute for the other raw materials. Perhaps a person has no vocation, perhaps he does not have children, a good marriage or deep friendships, but at least he can carry his head high in the world. Why he feels entitled to carry his head high depends on his ethical priorities. The reason might have to do with putting more into the world than he takes out, with taking responsibility for people who depend on him, with following the dictates of his faith. One way or another, it is a matter of meeting standards of conduct that he values. Social philosopher Michael Walzer put it memorably when he contrasted self-esteem with self-respect. We can feel self-esteem if enough other people tell us flattering things about ourselves, Walzer observed, but others cannot convince us that we have self-respect: "Now conscience is the court, and conscience is a shared knowledge, an internalized acceptance of community standards. . . . [W]e can't ignore the standards, and we can't juggle the verdict. We do measure up, or we don't."[5]

Intimate relationships with other humans, a satisfying vocation, and self-respect: These, I propose, are the active ingredients in achieving lasting and justified satisfaction with life as a whole.[6] The institutions for achieving these conditions are family, community, and workplace.[7] Seen in that light, one of the chief functions of government in enabling the pursuit of happiness is to ensure the vitality of those three institutions.

The Nature of Man as a Social Being

Whenever people propose policies and predict their effects, they are making assumptions about human nature. I make certain assumptions when I argue that the Plan will work. These assumptions about human nature are seldom stated explicitly, because often they bear no relationship to real human beings in real social groups. Consider the slogan, "From each according to his ability, to each according to his needs," that inspired generations of socialists. The slogan sounds wonderful, but even socialists knew that real human beings in large numbers wouldn't behave that way. Thus it is no accident that socialist theory held that the right social and economic institutions would change human nature. Socialism not only promised a "new man," it *required* a new man.

I contend that the Plan would work because it is congruent with human nature as it actually exists. These are the three key characteristics of human nature I have in mind:

- Humans as individuals tend to act in ways that advance their own interests.

- Humans tend to have a desire for approbation from other human beings.

- Humans tend to take on responsibilities to the extent that circumstances require them to do so.

I use the word *tend* in all three instances. Exceptions exist, but the tendencies are so pronounced and so widespread that if you are trying to predict the outcomes from complex policy changes, you may reliably expect that these characteristics of human beings will be at work. A few words of elaboration about each:

Humans as individuals tend to act in ways that advance their own interests. This is about as basic as truths about human behavior come, but it should not be confused with the false idea that human beings consistently try to maximize their interests. People more commonly "satisfice," to use Herbert Simon's word, contenting themselves with less than the last drop that they could have squeezed out of their situation.[8] Humans also do not act exclusively in their own self-interest. Altruism is everywhere. Human beings reliably pursue self-interest and reliably respond to incentives, but with moderation—that's the sense of my proposition.

Humans tend to be social creatures, having an innate desire for approbation from other human beings. Philosophers have argued for centuries about whether man has an innate moral sense.[9] But Adam Smith made a more limited argument that enables us to sidestep the most difficult questions about the moral sense. In *The Theory of Moral Sentiments*, Smith invokes the image of a man raised alone on a desert island without any communication with another human being. Such a man could not possibly think of his own character, Smith pointed out, any more than he could think of his face as being handsome. He would lack any frame of reference. But put him together with other human beings and he cannot avoid having a frame of reference for considering his own character, just as he cannot avoid having a frame of reference for assessing whether he is handsome. Smith's subsequent argument comes down to the proposition that man was formed for society by an "original desire to please, and an original aversion to offend," feeling pleasure from approbation for its own sake and pain from disapprobation. These reinforcements may be in the form of fame and fortune, in the good opinion of coworkers or neighbors, in the praise of one's boss, or in the admiration of one's children.[10]

The desire for approbation is a de facto moral sense. Communities function better when people exhibit cooperativeness; behaviors that are cooperative tend to receive approbation; we behave cooperatively to get approbation. John Adams nearly paraphrased Smith, writing in 1790 that "as Nature intended men for society, she has endowed them with passions, appetites and propensities calculated . . . to render them useful to each other in their social connections." Of these passions, appetites, and propensities, Adams continued, none was more essential and remarkable than the desire of every man "to be observed, considered, esteemed, praised, beloved, and admired by his fellows."[11] To a twenty-first-century reader, there is nothing strange in the thought, even if there may be in the wording. It seems to be an empirical fact. People like to be thought well of, and this can be a powerful force for making civil society work without compulsion.

Humans tend to take on responsibilities to the extent that circumstances require them to do so. This proposition applies to behaviors small and large. If someone else will wash the dishes, we tend to let them; if someone else will feed the hungry, we tend to let them; if someone else will defend the nation, we tend to let them. But when we are told, "If you don't do it, no one else will," we also tend to respond. If you think this is too optimistic a view of human behavior, test it against your own life. Try to think of something that matters to you, that will not get done if you don't do it, and that you nonetheless will take no steps to do. You will have a hard time coming up with an example. If it is really true that you want the thing to be done, and that you are in a position to do it, and no one else will—you will do it.

I specified "really true" in that claim because there are all sorts of things that we would like to see done but to which we can contribute only symbolically. Feeding the hungry is a good example. The probability that I will take action if I learn that one of my neighbors needs food is 100 percent. The probability that I will support a soup kitchen in my community is 100 percent if my church runs it; still high if it is a soup kitchen run by people in my community; and small if we are talking about a consortium of soup kitchens serving the Middle Atlantic states. The probability that I will voluntarily contribute extra taxes to the food stamp program is zero. Our willingness to assume responsibilities is intimately linked to the effect that we as individuals believe we can have.

This chapter has run through many ideas at a high level of generality. But as I spell out my expectations for the Plan in the chapters to come, these ideas are where the expectations come from. The real purpose of the Plan is the revitalization of the institutions that enable us to lead satisfying lives. The next three chapters take up the ways in which it would do so for the pivotal institutions known as vocation, family, and community.

9

Vocation

A central satisfaction of life comes from the sense of doing something one values and doing it well. Being engaged in that activity regularly means that one has a vocation. A few people know early in their lives that they are called to a vocation, whether to be priests or cellists or farmers or mothers. More commonly, people come to a vocation by trial and error.

For many people, the job never becomes a vocation. Sometimes these people find a surrogate elsewhere, through an avocation or involvement in the community. The Plan can help generate these sources of satisfaction as well, as described in chapter 11. But the topic of this chapter is vocation through the job. The role the Plan plays is twofold. The Plan makes it easier to find a vocation by changing jobs, and easier for a person to accumulate the capital to pursue a dream.

Changing Jobs

Few teenagers finish high school already knowing what job will make them happy. Or they may think they know, but change their minds. This is as true of those who go to college as those who do not—that's why students change their majors so often. The process of finding a job that makes one happy often continues well into a person's twenties, if not beyond. Only for a lucky few does it mean finding the perfect job. Some people find that working outdoors makes otherwise mundane jobs attractive. For others, working at home has the same effect. Jobs vary along many dimensions, and the history of most people who find satisfaction in a job is one of incrementally improving their situation over a period of years. This typically has meant changing employers and moving geographically.

Europe is especially useful as the canary in this part of the coal mine. Government regulation has made the costs of hiring an employee so high, and made it so hard to dismiss an employee, that the European labor market has become rigid. New jobs are scarce, and long-term unemployment is high. So an employee who has a job he hates nonetheless will tend to keep it rather than quit and look for a better one. European peasants used to be tied to the land. In this new version of serfdom, European workers are tied to their jobs.

A major strength of the American economy is its history of high labor mobility. As in other aspects of the welfare state, however, the United States is on the

European track. The Plan does nothing about one of the main sources of increasing immobility—the regulatory mandates that increasingly constrain the hiring and firing process—but it does promote freedom to move from job to job.

The main effect follows from the widespread reductions the Plan will produce in job-related medical coverage and retirement plans. Consider the situation facing a low- or middle-income worker who is not happy in his job under the current system. He might be willing to go without a salary for a few months, but going uninsured and perhaps having to give up retirement benefits that are not yet vested make the price of leaving too high. Under the Plan, millions more people will have portable retirement accounts and medical insurance. By the same token, the freedom of millions more people to look for a better job will be increased, and this is an essential part of incrementally finding a vocation.

The same effect will be felt by people who are out of the labor market altogether. Consider a single mother who has successfully gotten TANF, housing assistance, Medicaid, and food stamps in a city where the job market is bad. For her to pull up stakes and move to a city where the job market is better is foolish. If she doesn't find a job, she will have to go through the whole uncertain and stressful application process again and survive all its delays before she begins to get renewed support. Under the Plan, she faces none of those costs. Government no longer ties her to a place.

Pursuing the Dream

When introducing the Plan, I acknowledged that it could be implemented with requirements for contributions to retirement, but said that I thought it would be better without that requirement. We have come to one reason why: The Plan gives people a way of accumulating enough money to try to realize their ambitions—to go to college after all, even though they've got a family to support; to start their own business; to leave Dubuque and move to Alaska. The dreams can take numberless variations, but people working in low-income jobs and responsible for families usually have to abandon them. The Plan does not make such dreams easy to realize, but it does bring them into the realm of the possible, given discipline and hard work.

That last proviso—"given discipline and hard work"—points to one of the ways in which the Plan is likely to have positive side effects. The Plan does not provide enough money in any one year to finance much of anything. It does provide enough money so that someone can save over the course of three or four years, then go to the bank and say, "Here is what I have done, planning for this day, and how much I have accumulated," and thereby have a chance of getting a loan. That prospect, and the experience of saving over those years, are themselves valuable outcomes. The Plan will expand that prospect to millions of people who have never considered it before. Within those millions, some subset will acquire habits of self-discipline and long-term planning that will positively affect their lives on many dimensions.

And, not incidentally, many within that subset will succeed in achieving their original dream.

That leads to the question of those who try and fail. They save for four years, get a loan, start that cherished new business—and it fails. Has the Plan's effect been good or bad? Reasonable people will disagree. My position is that failure is a positive part of life. The cliché about learning more from our failures than our successes is true. The cliché that some of the best things in our lives come about because of failure is true. The cliché that life is not a destination but a journey is true. If the Plan enables millions of people to pursue their dreams who would not have been able to pursue them otherwise, I count that as a success in itself. And for those who have failed, the Plan continues to provide a backstop. They have lost the money that went into their venture, but they still have the grant, plus whatever they can make from a job, to pick themselves back up again.

Others will disagree, valuing security more than I do. There is no disputing tastes, but this thought is relevant: If you are a person who values security above all else, the Plan gives you the option of being as conservative as you wish—putting all of your retirement money into bonds instead of stocks; paying for a health-care plan that leaves no chance whatsoever that you will be left uncovered for anything. But why dictate that everyone must behave as you do? Why not let people decide for themselves how they want to live their lives? If they make mistakes, they will have been their mistakes, not yours. Those who want to impose security on others have no idea whether they are doing the right thing for someone else's ultimate happiness. They shouldn't have the right to do so.

The opportunity to try different paths is at the heart of acquiring a vocation. It is one of the greatest advantages that youths from economically secure families enjoy. The Plan goes a long way toward extending that opportunity to everyone.

10

Marriage

The Plan's effects on marriage fall into two categories: effects on the decision to marry, and effects on people after they are married.

Effects on the Decision to Marry

The broadest effect of the Plan is to make marriage economically easier for low-income people. If this effect were to play out uniformly across different types of people, it would produce good marriages and bad in proportions that are hard to forecast in advance. But it will not play out uniformly. The Plan's greatest effect will be on those couples who worry about money before deciding to get married, and its smallest effect will be on those who get married on a whim. Or, to put it another way, the Plan will have the most effect on the most responsible young people and the least effect on the least responsible, producing a strong bias toward enabling good marriages to occur.[1]

But just because the Plan makes marriage easier does not necessarily mean that large numbers of people will choose to marry who do not marry now. So let us consider more specifically how the Plan affects the choice to marry, cohabit, live separately, or end a relationship.

In trying to think through how the changed incentives will play out, much depends on the answer to one question: How much difference does marriage make to a father's legal rights and obligations toward the child he fathers? At one extreme is a marriage-doesn't-count regime in which the standing of the unmarried biological father is identical to the standing of the married biological father. At the other extreme is a marriage-is-everything regime in which the biological father of a child has no legal rights and no legal obligations regarding his child unless he marries—close to the de facto framework for marriage that applied in the United States and Europe until the 1960s.[2]

If marriage doesn't count, the Plan has no effect on the decision to marry. It adds money to the income of both of the partners, but it does not change the vectors of the economic incentives compared to the current system. If marriage doesn't matter legally, the decision to marry is based exclusively on noneconomic considerations

Under a marriage-is-everything regime, the effects of the Plan on marriage are radically different. The woman knows she must marry to have any claim on the father of her children. She also knows that even an unemployed boyfriend has

$7,000 in visible cash income (as always, assuming $3,000 is going to health care). If she becomes pregnant, this provides her with a strong incentive to marry. That same $7,000 in visible income gives a reluctant boyfriend an extra incentive to avoid marriage. Those are the same competing incentives that used to apply in the United States when the legal regime was effectively marriage-is-everything and the welfare state was still small. The result in that era was that women actively avoided becoming pregnant without the assurance of marriage, and the percentage of children born out of wedlock was in the low single digits. Comparable dynamics are fostered by the Plan under a marriage-is-everything regime.

If the nation moves toward a marriage-doesn't-count regime, it is hard to see how the Plan makes matters worse. Cohabitation will continue to spread, but the Plan doesn't make marriage less desirable.[3] If the nation moves toward restoring the unique obligations associated with marriage, the Plan would provide a powerful incentive for a woman to require marriage before bearing a man's child. It is hard to think of any other single change that would have as many positive effects on the next generation of children.[4]

Effects on Marriage among the Married

Whatever happens to the laws surrounding marriage, large numbers of people will continue to get married. The effects of the Plan on existing marriages are limited to families for whom the cash grant is an important part of total family income. They are of four kinds: effects on divorce; effects that make it easier for mothers to have both children and a career; effects that make it easier for mothers to stay at home; and effects that increase the autonomy and responsibility of the family as a unit.

Effects on divorce. Under the current system, women who forgo careers to be full-time housewives and mothers are vulnerable to being forced into the labor market in midlife without job skills or experience. For affluent couples, this vulnerability is counterbalanced by adequate alimony and child support. The Plan provides a similar counterbalance for women in low-income and middle-income households. One may be opposed to divorce and yet in favor of measures that free women from the economic compulsion to remain in a bad marriage. On the other side of the ledger, the Plan's financial guarantee will make it easier for salvageable marriages to break up. I know of no way to forecast what the mix will be.

Effects that make it easier for mothers to have both children and a career. As I tackle the delicate topic of whether mothers stay at home or have a job outside the home, the crucial distinction is between mothers who work because they like their jobs and those who work out of economic necessity. For now, I am referring exclusively to mothers who prefer to work outside the home.

Mothers in affluent households who want to work outside the home hire nannies or send their children to good day-care centers. The Plan makes it easier for mothers in low-income and middle-income households to do the same thing. For families in which the woman is already working, the Plan will ease the financial strain of paying for child care. For families in which the woman is not working but wants to, the Plan will enable her to do so by providing resources for buying child care. I interpret both effects as being good for the marriages in question.[5] The Plan does nothing to persuade mothers with children to work outside the home. It makes it easier for them to do so if they want to.

Effects that make it easier for mothers to stay home. Now the issue is the mother who is working out of economic necessity, but, given the option, would rather work part-time or be a full-time housewife and mother. Once again, the Plan is not going to affect the decisions of women in affluent households for whom the grant is a negligible percentage of the family's income. But the Plan is likely to have large effects on households with incomes well into the middle class.

To see why the importance of the Plan reaches so far up the income ladder, remember that a woman who does not work gets the cash grant no matter how much her husband makes. For many women with young children who work only because they have to help make ends meet, the grant can easily represent the difference between financial hardship and being able to get along on the husband's income alone. In a household where the husband makes, say, $50,000 and the wife makes $25,000, a number of financial obligations are likely to be in place when a child arrives that make it difficult to get along on $50,000. So the wife continues to work, except that now she must pay (let's say) $5,000 a year for day care, and the family gets along on an income of $70,000. The Plan makes it easier to tweak the family finances so that the wife can quit her job if she wishes. In this specific instance, the family may not find it feasible to go from a family income of $70,000 to $50,000, but they could manage to go from $70,000 to $59,000.[6] As the family's income level goes down, all of these effects of the cash grant get larger. Insofar as the Plan permits more women to do what they prefer to do regarding a central life role—mother—it is unambiguously positive for those women and positive for the children as well.

More mothers staying at home because they choose to do so will also be good for marriage.[7] A marriage can be filled with family activities or it can be stripped down. The more time that is filled by careers, the more stripping-down of family life has to occur. It is not a matter of choice. Weekends are a different kind of experience in a family where all the domestic chores of the week must be crowded into Saturday and Sunday versus one where they are not. The availability for volunteer work at the local school differs between those two households. The availability to be a neighbor in times of need differs. The availability to care for aging parents differs. The availability to be a Sunday school teacher differs. All of these activities on the part of either parent are in addition to the childrearing activities that can fill a marriage or be stripped down. It is a simple relationship: The more resources that are devoted to a marriage, the richer that marriage is likely to be.

The richer the marriages in a community, the more the community thrives. The Plan's effect on enabling wives to stay home if they wish could be one of its most important ones.

Effects that make the family more autonomous and responsible. The Plan returns core functions and responsibilities to the family, and doing so is likely to have a revitalizing effect on the institution as a whole.

Consider this paradox: Taking on a wife and then becoming a father is what a young man, full of wild oats, should least like to do. And yet throughout history and across cultures, young men have yearned to marry. In some cultures, they have scrimped and saved to accumulate bride prices. In our own culture until well into the twentieth century, young men consciously behaved in ways that demonstrated they would be good providers so that they could convince a woman to marry them. Why have young men so consistently acted against what their hormones would lead them to do in a state of nature?

The direct answer is that marriage used to be the only way that most men could get regular sexual access to a woman—a powerful incentive. But that only pushes the question back further. Why should women have so consistently withheld sexual access until marriage? Again there is a direct answer: The woman was left holding the baby. Before the advent of the welfare state, women could not afford the risk of sex without a commitment from the man.

If that were the full explanation of why young men yearned to marry, the Plan wouldn't make any difference.

Nothing is going to repeal the sexual revolution, and the Plan provides a woman with the resources to raise a child on her own if necessary. But the bald biological and economic incentives I just described are only part of the explanation. Over the eons required for us to become *Homo sapiens*, humans living in demanding environments had a survival advantage if the man stuck around after they mated, suggesting that by this time a male's genetic makeup contains predispositions not only to sow wild oats, but also to be a family man. Whether he ever becomes a family man depends on how culture mediates these competing impulses.

Historically, culture has taken the incentives I just described and pieced together a narrative around them consisting of norms, rewards, and punishments. In the case of young males, most cultures provided for a period of sowing wild oats but also said to them that the way to enter the fraternity of men was by becoming a husband and father. That message was based on a truth: the welfare of the community depended upon the formation of stable families. Being a husband and father became the badge of being an adult male because those roles were laden with responsibilities and obligations.

Now consider the phrase that is so often applied to social welfare systems: the *safety net*. It is wonderfully apt. People who know that a net is below them do reckless things that they wouldn't do otherwise. Under the current system, the net is there regardless of how people behave. Under the Plan, people have ample raw materials for a net, but they must weave it for themselves. People have to make choices, and it is possible to make the wrong choices. The potential rewards from marriage increase for low-income men and women because the economic assets they bring to the marriage increase. Each partner brings resources that, combined and used prudently, give them the prospect of a bright and secure future. Similarly, the potential risks increase: Men and women alike have more to lose economically if their prospective spouses are irresponsible. I do not mean to sound naïve. People have made bad marriage choices throughout history and will continue to do so under any social regime. But the Plan restores some of the traditional narrative that in the past led people to look beyond short-term sexual attraction and think about long-term effects.

Under the Plan, everyone still has the option of remaining single, moving in and out of relationships. But most people want something deeper and more lasting than that, something that looks like marriage traditionally defined. Under the Plan, marriage once again becomes the locus within which a man and woman can make a future together, laden with responsibilities and obligations that cannot be put aside.

I have provided a number of scenarios without any way to estimate which ones are the most likely. My own conclusion is based on a few core propositions that fall from the discussion in chapter 8, applied here to marriage:

- The yearning for a lasting, intimate sexual relationship is hardwired into both women and men. Sexual proclivities among men and women differ in many ways, but both sexes want a mate.

- The current decline in marriage is not a function of modernity, but of the welfare state. The welfare state systematically competes with the natural attraction to marriage.

- To restore the vitality of marriage, it is not necessary that policy do anything to encourage marriage. Policy simply needs to stop getting in the way.

- The Plan stops policy from getting in the way.

If these propositions are not correct, the Plan leaves marriage no worse off than it is now. If they are correct, the Plan will give marriage renewed meaning and vitality.

11

Community

The effects of the Plan on vocation and family will be substantial, but the effects on civil life will be transforming. As the government's role in American life spread during the last seventy years, it crowded out America's most effective resource for dealing with human needs. The Plan returns the stuff of life to the hands of civil society.

Here is Alexis de Tocqueville on the American genius for voluntary association:

> Americans of all ages, all stations in life, and all types of dispositions are forever forming associations. There are not only commercial and industrial associations in which all take part, but others of a thousand different types—religious, moral, serious, futile, very general and very limited, immensely large and very minute.

Americans combine to give fêtes, found seminaries, build churches, distribute books, and send missionaries to the antipodes. Hospitals, prisons, and schools take place in that way. Finally, if they want to proclaim a truth or propagate some feeling by the encouragement of a great example, they form an association. In every case, at the head of any new undertaking, where in France you would find the government or in England some territorial magnate, in the United States you are sure to find an association.[1]

The tradition continues today, evident in private philanthropic endeavors that are much rarer in Europe, and in the continuing social and religious organizations that are still an important part of life in working-class and middle-class America. But much has changed as well, for reasons that Tocqueville anticipated:

A government could take the place of some of the largest associations in America, and some particular states of the Union have already attempted that. But what political power could ever carry on the vast multitude of lesser undertakings which associations daily enable American citizens to control? . . . The more government takes the place of associations, the more will individuals lose the idea of forming associations and need the government to come to their help. That is a vicious circle of cause and effect.[2]

The simple number of associations continues to increase to this day. But the newcomers are no longer associations that take on social tasks for themselves. Rather, they are advocacy groups that seek to influence how the government will do those tasks.[3] The experience of voluntary associations based on broad memberships that actually performed the social tasks vindicated Tocqueville's prediction. They were still growing into the 1920s. Then their membership declined precipitously.[4]

This is not the place to untangle all the ways in which changes in American society affected voluntary associations, but two large events are among them. First came the 1935 Social Security Act, which created both Social Security and Aid to Families with Dependent Children. Each program took what had been a major arena of private activity unto the federal government. Thirty years later came Lyndon Johnson's Great Society and the proliferation of social programs that accompanied it, proclaiming in effect that there was no longer any aspect of poverty and deprivation that the federal government would not take the lead in solving.

To convey what has been lost, it is necessary to tell the story of how extensive civic participation used to be. It begins with the network of fraternal associations for dealing with misfortune or old age through mutual insurance, such as the Odd Fellows, Elks, Masons, Moose, Redmen, and Knights of Pythias. Some were organized around specific occupations. Some were linked to membership in an ethnic group—Hebrew, Irish, Italian. Most of the associations run by whites excluded blacks in those years, but that did not keep blacks from just as energetically developing their own fraternal associations.[5]

Few people today realize the size and reach of these networks. In the mid-1920s, the National Fraternal Congress had 120,000 lodges.[6] The Odd Fellows had about 16 million members and the Knights of Pythias about 6 million.[7] So extensive were the fraternal organizations that an official of the New Hampshire Bureau of Labor could write in 1894 that "the tendency to join fraternal organizations for the purpose of obtaining care and relief in the event of sickness and insurance for the family in case of death is well-nigh universal."[8] Today, the remnants of these fraternal organizations perform shadows of their former functions.

Besides their mutual insurance functions, the fraternal organizations supported extensive social service activities. In that task they were supplemented by a long list of other charities exclusively focused on assistance to nonmembers. It is difficult to convey the magnitude of the effort to help the poor prior to the advent of the welfare state because that effort was so decentralized, but consider just a few statistics from New York City at the turn of the twentieth century. Here is the roster of activities discovered in a survey of 112 Protestant churches in Manhattan and the Bronx: forty-eight industrial schools, forty-five libraries or reading rooms, forty-four sewing schools, forty kindergartens, twenty-nine small-sum savings banks and loan associations, twenty-one employment offices, twenty gymnasia and swimming pools, eight medical dispensaries, seven full-day nurseries, and four lodging houses.[9]

Those are just some of the Protestant churches in two boroughs of New York City, and it is not a complete list of the activities shown in the report. Now suppose I could add (I do not have the data) the activities in the other boroughs.

Then add the activities of the rest of the Protestant churches. Then add the activities of the New York Catholic diocese. Then add those of the Jewish charities. And, after all that, suppose I could tally the activities of a completely separate and extensive web of *secular* voluntary associations. Perhaps the numbers from a very different setting will indicate how long that list might have been: When one small midwestern state, Iowa, mounted a food conservation program in World War I, it engaged the participation of 2,873 church congregations and 9,630 chapters of thirty-one different secular fraternal associations.[10]

In evaluating such evidence, two issues must be separated. If the question is whether the philanthropic network successfully dealt with all the human needs that existed, the answer is obviously no. Dire poverty existed in the presence of all this activity. But that's not the right question. The assistance was being given in the context of national wealth that in 1900 amounted to a per-capita gross domestic product (GDP) of about $5,400 in today's dollars, and about two-thirds of the nation's nonfarm families were below the poverty line as presently defined.[11] I must put it as an assertion because the aggregate numbers for philanthropy in New York City cannot be accurately estimated, but I think it is a safe assertion: New York City's tax base in 1900 could not have funded anything approaching the level of philanthropic activities—cash and services combined—that were provided voluntarily.

Some perspective on this issue is provided by Jacob Riis, whose iconic photographs of the slums of New York documented all that was most terrible about poverty in that era. Today, Riis's work is often used to illustrate the brutality of the Industrial Revolution. Here is the same Jacob Riis, in the same book with those photographs, writing about New York City's response:

> Nowhere is there so eager a readiness to help . . . nowhere are such armies of devoted workers. . . . [New York's] poverty, its slums, and its suffering are the result of unprecedented growth with the consequent disorder and crowding, and the common penalty of metropolitan greatness. . . . [T]he thousand and one charities that in one way or another reach the homes and the lives of the poor with sweetening touch, are proof that if much is yet to be done, if the need only grows with the effort, hearts and hands will be found to do it in ever-increasing measure.[12]

The correct question to ask about dealing with human needs in the twenty-first century is: What if the same proportional level of effort went into civil society's efforts to deal with human needs *at today's level of national wealth?*

I urge interested readers to pursue the story of the voluntary associations—they represent an extraordinary, largely forgotten accomplishment.[13] Here, I make a limited point. At the time the New Deal began, mutual assistance for insurance did not consist of a few isolated workingmen's groups. Philanthropy to the poor did not consist of a few Lady Bountifuls distributing food baskets. Broad networks, engaging people from the top to bottom of society, spontaneously formed by ordinary citizens, provided sophisticated and effective social insurance and social services of every sort. They did so not just in rural towns or small cities, but in the largest and most impersonal of megalopolises. When I express confidence that under the Plan such networks will regenerate, it is based on historical precedent about how Americans left to themselves tackle social needs, not on wishful thinking.

This leaves open the question of whether it is better to let civil society handle these efforts. It may be argued that it is better to have paid bureaucracies deal with social problems. That way, the burden is not left to people who choose to help, but shared among all the taxpayers. Furthermore, it is more convenient to have bureaucracies do it. Being a part-time social worker appeals to some people, but most of us would rather pay our taxes and be done with it. Perhaps we should concentrate on improving the government bureaucracies that deal with these problems, not dismantling them.

The benefits of returning these functions to civil society are of two kinds: Benefits for the recipients of assistance, and benefits for the rest of us.

The Benefits for Recipients

People trying to help those in need must struggle with a dilemma that the economists call *moral hazard*. People who are in need through no fault of their own can be given generous assistance with no downside risk. But people who are in need at least partly because of their own behavior pose a problem: How to relieve their distress without making it more likely that they will continue to behave in the ways that brought on their difficulties, and without sending the wrong signal to other people who might be tempted.

Bureaucracies have no answer to this dilemma. They cannot distinguish between people who need a pat on the back and those who need a stern warning. They cannot provide help to people who have behaved irresponsibly in a way that does not make it easier for others to behave irresponsibly. Bureaucracies must by their nature be morally indifferent. Indeed, the advocates of the welfare state hold up the moral neutrality of the bureaucracy as one of its advantages because aid is provided without stigma. In contrast, not only are private organizations free to combine moral instruction with the help they give, but such moral instruction is often a primary motivation for the people who are doing the work. Religious belief is sometimes its basis, but the point of view emerges in secular organizations as well. If the recipients of the help are approached as independent moral agents, and if their behavior has contributed to their problems, then the provision of assistance *must* be linked with attempts to get them to change their ways, subtle or overt.

The result is that private philanthropies tend to provide help in ways that minimize moral hazard. Sometimes moral hazard is reduced because a social penalty accompanies the help—the Florence Crittendon Homes for unwed mothers, for instance, provided help, but moral neutrality about getting pregnant without a husband was not part of the package. Sometimes moral hazard is reduced because the outlook and behavior of the person receiving the assistance are changed for the better. In either case, private charities have the advantage over bureaucracies if the objective is not just to minister to needs, but to discourage the need from arising.

Bureaucracies are also inferior to private philanthropy because a bureaucracy's highest interest cannot help being its own welfare. A new employee may enter a bureaucracy as idealistic as any volunteer, but those who thrive and advance will be those who advance the bureaucracy's interests most effectively. In the business sector, that means growing by gaining new customers and being profitable. For a government bureaucracy, it means growing by increasing its budget and staff.

The institutional interests that drove private philanthropy before the government took a role were the opposite. Charitable organizations had to attract volunteers and donors. The way to attract volunteers was by providing satisfying work for volunteers—which meant the kind of work that the organization was set up to do in the first place, not bureaucratic paper shuffling. The way to attract donors was being able to assure them that their money went to the organization's clients, not to support a large administrative staff. Private charitable organizations had no choice but to keep the effectiveness of their work at the forefront of their attention, else they would go out of business.

It is possible to destroy these advantages of private organizations. The United Way seems designed to make supporting charitable services as much like paying taxes as possible. Go to the Ford Foundation, Red Cross, or other philanthropies with large guaranteed incomes, and you will usually find splendid executive offices, bloated administrative staffs, and layers of paperwork. Go instead to the Salvation Army or any philanthropy that relies on volunteers and a steady stream of small incoming donations, and you will tend to find lean administrative staffs and a continuing focus on the recipients of the assistance.[14]

The Benefits for the Rest of Us

The second large benefit of taking these functions back into our own hands is that turning them over to a bureaucracy means turning over too much of the stuff of life to them. By *stuff of life* I mean the elemental events of birth, death, growing up, raising children, comforting the bereaved, celebrating success, dealing with adversity, applauding the good, and scorning the bad—coping with life as it exists around us in all its richness. The chief defect of the welfare state from this perspective is not that it is inefficient in dealing with social needs (though it often is), nor that it is ineffectual in dealing with them (though it often is), nor even that it often exacerbates the very problems it is supposed to solve (as it often does). The welfare state drains too much of the life from life.

This argument is not an exhortation for us all to become social workers in our spare time. Give the functions back to the community, and enough people will respond. Free riders can be tolerated. Rather, the existence of vital, extensive networks of voluntary associations engaged in dealing with basic social needs benefits all of us for two other reasons.

The first reason is that such networks are an indispensable way for virtue to be inculcated and practiced in the next generation, and the transmission of virtue is the indispensable task of a free society.

The link between virtue and the success of a free society is not theoretical, but tangible and immediate. A free market cannot work unless the overwhelming majority of the population practices good faith in business transactions. Allowing people to adopt any lifestyle they prefer will not work if a culture does not socialize an overwhelming majority of its children to take responsibility for their actions, to understand long-term consequences, and to exercise self-restraint. Ultimately, a free society does not work unless the population shares a basic sense of right and wrong based on virtue classically understood, propounded in similar terms by thinkers as culturally dissimilar as Aristotle and Confucius. As Edmund Burke put it, "Men are qualified for civil liberty in exact proportion to their disposition to put moral chains upon their own appetites. ... . It is ordained in the eternal constitution of things that men of intemperate minds cannot be free. Their passions forge their fetters."[15]

The question then becomes how virtue is acquired. Aristotle's answer is still the right one: Virtue has the characteristics of a habit and of an acquired skill. It is not enough to tell children that they should be honest, compassionate, and generous. They must *practice* honesty, compassion, and generosity in the same way that they practice a musical instrument or a sport. Nor does the need for practice stop with childhood. People who behave honestly, compassionately, and generously do not think about each individual choice and decide whether in this particular instance to be honest, compassionate, or generous. They do it as a habit.

If this is an accurate description of how virtue is acquired, then transferring human problems to bureaucracies has an indirect consequence that ultimately degrades the society as a whole: Doing so shrinks an arena in which virtues such as generosity and compassion are practiced. It may not be necessary for everyone to become a volunteer social worker to find satisfaction in life, but it is important that people deal with the human needs of others in a way that is an integral part of everyone's life. In a society where the responsibility for coping with human needs is consigned to bureaucracies, the development of virtue in the next generation is impeded. In a society where that responsibility remains with ordinary citizens, the development of virtue in the next generation is invigorated.[16]

The other reason that the stuff of life should not be handed over to bureaucracies involves the dynamics through which communities remain vital or become moribund. Broken down into constituent parts, vital communities consist of a multitude of affiliations among people who are drawn to engage with one another. Some of these affiliations are as simple as shopping at a local store; some are intended for nothing more than a good time—the backyard barbecue. Some are organizational—serving as a deacon in one's church. The kinds of affiliations that draw communities together and give them vitality are tendrils that require something to attach themselves to, some core of functions around which the affiliations that constitute a vital community can form and grow. When the government takes away a core function, it takes away one of the poles for those tendrils. By hiring professional social workers to care for those most in need, it cuts off nourishment to secondary and tertiary behaviors that have nothing to do with social work. According to the logic of the social engineer, there is no causal connection between such apparently disparate events as the establishment of a welfare bureaucracy and the reduced likelihood (after the passage of some years) that, when someone dies, a neighbor will prepare a casserole for the bereaved family's dinner. According to the logic I am using, there is a causal connection of great importance.

These are my reasons for thinking that the effects of the Plan on civic life will be transforming. The grant will put in each individual's hands the means to take care of himself under ordinary circumstances. But some will not take care of themselves. Sometimes the reasons will be beyond their control. Sometimes the reasons will stem from fecklessness. Most reasons will be somewhere in between. The responses to the needs posed by these cases will be as flexible as their causes. The level of wealth available to address these needs will dwarf the resources that were available to the fraternal and philanthropic networks of a century ago. Nothing stands in the way of the restoration of networks that are appropriate and generous, and that actually solve problems, except the will to put the responsibility for those problems back in our hands.

12

Conclusion

I began this thought experiment by asking you to ignore that the Plan was politically impossible today. I end it by proposing that something very like the Plan is politically inevitable—not next year, but sometime. Two historical forces lead me to this conclusion.

The first is the secular increase in wealth as the American economy just keeps on growing. Figure 4 on the next page shows the history of American GDP since 1900. We may fret about this year's unemployment rate and the effect of a hike in interest rates on economic growth next year, or we may be convinced that the current administration is the best or worst thing to happen to American economic policy in years, but all of the short-term considerations are swamped by this long-term truth: Real per-capita GDP has grown with remarkable fidelity to an exponential growth equation for more than a century. It is, of course, possible to elect leaders so incompetent that they will do to the American

FIGURE 4

AMERICAN GROSS DOMESTIC PRODUCT, 1900–2004

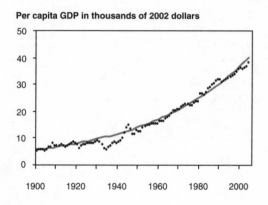

Per capita GDP in thousands of 2002 dollars

SOURCE: 1900–1959, U.S. Bureau of the Census (1975), Table F 1–5. 1960–2000, U.S. Bureau of the Census (2005b), Table 641, and comparable tables in earlier editions.

economy what the Soviet leaders did to theirs, but, short of that, we are probably going to watch wealth increase in the decades to come. That curve cannot keep going up for much longer without it becoming obvious to a consensus of the American electorate that lack of money cannot be the reason we have poverty, lack of medical coverage, or an underclass. The problem is that we are spending the money badly.

The second great historical force is the limited competence of government—not our government in particular, or the welfare state in particular, but any government. The limits do not arise because bureaucrats are lazy or the laws improperly written, but from truths about what human beings do when they are not forced to behave in ways that elicit the voluntary cooperation of other people. If constructed with great care, it is possible to have a government that administers a competent army, competent police, and competent courts. Even accomplishing this much is not easy. Every step beyond these simplest, most basic tasks is fraught with increasing difficulty. By the time the government begins trying to administer to complex human needs, it is far out of its depth. Individuals and groups acting privately, with no choice but to behave in ways that elicit voluntary cooperation, do these jobs better. The limited competence of government is inherent. At some point in this century, that too will become a consensus understanding.

Once enough people recognize these realities, the way will be open for reform. What was clear to the Founders will once again become clear to a future generation: The greatness of the American project was that it set out to let everyone live life as each person saw fit, as long as each accorded the same freedom to everyone else.

America could not reach that goal as long as the fatal flaw of slavery persisted. When the goal came into sight in the 1960s, we lost our focus and then lost ground. Sometime in the twenty-first century it will become possible to take up the task again, more expansively than the Founders could have dreamed but seeking the same end: taking our lives back into our own hands—*ours* as individuals, *ours* as families, and *ours* as communities.

APPENDIXES

Appendix A

The Programs to Be Eliminated

Income Transfers with Eligibility Independent of Earned Income

The first category of programs to be eliminated under the Plan comprises transfers that are not determined by income. The largest are the retirement programs, dominated by Social Security. Table A-1 on the following page lists all of these programs, which together cost more than $800 billion in 2002. Workers' compensation is included insofar as it involves state or federal payments of premiums or benefits. All of workers' compensation would be shifted (as most of it is now) to premiums and benefits paid by employers. I have excluded all retirement benefits for government workers from this calculation. If the Plan were to be enacted, some portion of those costs would appropriately be counted as costs of the current system (the pension system for government employees folds Social Security into its benefit package without calling it Social Security), but I have not tried to do that calculation.

TABLE A-1

INCOME TRANSFERS WITH ELIGIBILITY INDEPENDENT
OF EARNED INCOME

Program	Outlays in 2002 (in millions of dollars)
Retirement and disability insurance benefit payments	
Old age, survivors, and disability insurance	446,559
Railroad retirement and disability	8,698
Workers' compensation payments (federal and state)[a]	21,400
Other government disability insurance and retirement[b]	5,850
Medicare	263,750
Unemployment insurance benefit payments	
State unemployment insurance compensation	52,939
Unemployment compensation for federal civilian employees	327
Unemployment compensation for railroad employees	96
Unemployment compensation for veterans	325
Other unemployment compensation	287
TOTAL	**800,231**

SOURCE: U.S. Bureau of the Census (2005b), tables 519 and 541.
a. Includes state and federal premiums and state benefit payments in 2001, the most recent available year. Excludes premiums or benefits by private carriers or employers' self-insurance.
b. Excludes disability insurance and retirement for government employees, civilian or military.

Transfers of Income, In-Kind, and Services to Low-Income Individuals

Most of the transfers in this category are the legacy of the 1960s' War on Poverty, started then on a small scale and expanded over time. To identify these programs, listed in table A-2, I employ the standard compilation presented annually in the Census Bureau's *Statistical Abstract of the United States* under the title, "Cash and Noncash Benefits for Persons with Limited Income," table 524 in the 2004–2005 edition.

Transfers to Industry, Nonprofits, and Favored Groups

I have expanded the category often described as corporate welfare to include government spending that benefits an industry, corporation, nonprofit organization, or an identifiable group. Sometimes the group shares an occupation (for example, farmers), sometimes ethnicity (for example, American Indians), sometimes the same geographical setting (as in the case of the towns and cities selected for block grants). Sometimes the transfer is direct, in the form of grants, loans, or subsidies. In many cases the transfer is implicit, with the government funding a service or applied research for an industry that the industry should be doing for itself if the service or research is worth the cost.

Defining what programs fit into this category requires judgment calls. Compare expenditures on highways and Amtrak, for example. The category of people who benefit from highways is so close to universal that the expenditures can be deemed a public good rather than a transfer, and the taxes on gas and trucks go a long way toward skewing the costs toward those who get the most use from highways. In contrast, the subsidies to Amtrak benefit a comparatively

TABLE A-2

TRANSFERS FOR LOW-INCOME INDIVIDUALS

Program	Outlays in 2002 (in millions of dollars)		
	Federal	State and Local	Total
Medical care	163,760	118,708	282,468
Medicaid	146,643	111,573	258,216
Veterans	8,185	—	8,185
General assistance	—	4,956	4,956
State children's health insurance programs	3,776	1,631	5,407
Indian health services	2,758	—	2,758
Maternal and child health services	731	548	1,279
Consolidated health centers	1,328	—	1,328
Cash aid	82,476	19,681	102,157
Supplemental security income	33,871	4,651	38,522
Temporary assistance for needy families (TANF)	6,481	6,554	13,035
Earned income tax credit (refunded portion)	27,830	—	27,830
Foster care	4,523	4,095	8,618
Child tax credit (refunded portion)	5,060	—	5,060
General assistance	—	3,251	3,251
Pensions for needy veterans	3,177	—	3,177
Food benefits	36,824	2,482	39,306
Food stamps	21,657	2,397	24,054
School lunch program	6,064	—	6,064
Women, infants, and children	4,350	—	4,350
Child- and adult-care food program	1,638	—	1,638
School breakfast	1,515	—	1,515
Housing benefits	34,861	705	35,566
Low-income housing assistance (Section 8)	18,499	—	18,499
Low-rent public housing	8,213	—	8,213
Rural housing loans	3,499	—	3,499
Home investment partnerships	1,796	704	2,500
Housing for the elderly and disabled	3,499	—	3,499

(*continued on next page*)

(*Table A-2 continued*)	Outlays in 2002 (in millions of dollars)		
		State and	
Program	Federal	Local	Total
Education aid	28,783	1,701	30,484
Pell Grants	11,364	—	11,364
Head Start	6,538	1,634	8,172
Stafford loans	7,523	—	7,523
Federal Work-Study Program	1,000	—	1,000
Federal Trio Programs	827	—	827
Services	17,525	4,690	22,215
Social services (Title 20)	2,743	—	2,743
Child care for TANF recipients and ex-recipients	1,572	750	2,322
Child care and development block grants	6,383	2,206	8,589
TANF services	4,413	1,734	6,147
Homeless assistance grants	1,044	—	1,044
Jobs and training	6,893	915	7,808
TANF work activities	2,121	606	2,727
Training for disadvantaged adults and youth	1,950	—	1,950
Job Corps	1,532	—	1,532
Energy assistance	2,030	122	2,152
Low-income energy assistance	1,800	—	1,800
TOTAL	**373,152**	**149,004**	**522,156**

SOURCE: U.S. Bureau of the Census (2005b), table 524.

small and geographically defined population and therefore constitute a transfer. Or consider the many statistical and research bureaus funded by the government. I do not treat the data collected by the Bureau of Labor Statistics or the basic research funded by the National Institutes of Health as transfers. Such activities may or may not be a legitimate function of government, but at least an argument can be made that such information has such a generalized audience, or is so far removed from commercial applications, that it does not constitute a transfer. When, in contrast, the Agricultural Marketing Service collects data on agricultural commodity markets and publishes that information in *Market News*, it is doing something that directly benefits agricultural producers, processors, and distributors and that, in other industries, is routinely financed by the industry that needs the information.

The amounts of money involved are so small, comparatively speaking, that being right or wrong on the borderline cases makes no difference to the financial feasibility of the Plan. When Stephen Slivinski of the Cato Institute set out to identify corporate welfare, the programs he tagged had combined budgets of about $87 billion in 2001.[1] As large as this amount is in ordinary terms, it represents less than 7 percent of the total spent on the income transfers in the preceding two tables. I have contented myself with a subset of the programs he identified, adding one of my own (the Bureau of Indian Affairs), with total expenditures of about $63 billion. I have omitted many programs in Slivinski's list not because I think he was wrong, but because including them would arouse questions that are not worth debating in this context; the money involved is too small to have any bearing on the affordability of the Plan. In table A-3, I have attached short notes describing the transfers associated with some of the line items with the most innocuous names (such as "foreign assistance programs").

TABLE A-3

TRANSFERS TO INDUSTRY, NONPROFITS, AND FAVORED GROUPS

Program	Outlays in 2001 (in millions of dollars)
Department of Agriculture	
Agricultural Credit Insurance Fund	1,007
Agricultural Marketing Service	817
Agricultural Research Service	900
Commodity Credit Corporation	7,652
Commodity Price Supports	14,570
Conservation Reserve Program[a]	1,656
Cooperative State Research, Education, and Extension Service	1,020
Export Enhancement Program	478
Farm Service Agency[b]	896
Federal Crop Insurance Program	2,583
Foreign Assistance Programs[c]	1,295
Forest Service: State and Private Forestry[d]	363
Market Access Programs	123
National Agricultural Statistics Service	100
Natural Resource Conservation Service[e]	1,074
Rural Business-Cooperative Service	60
Rural Utilities Service	255
Rural Community Advancement Program	876
Department of Commerce	
Advanced Technology Program	132
Economic Development Administration	411
Information Infrastructure Grants	29
International Trade Administration	305
Manufacturing Extension Partnership[f]	109
Minority Business Development Agency	23
American Fisheries Promotion Act	6
National Marine Fisheries Service	735
Department of Defense	
Army Corps of Engineers[g]	2,285
Advanced Research Projects Agency	
Communications Systems and Communications Technology	334
Materials and Electronics Technology	264

(continued on next page)

(*Table A-3 continued*)

Program	Outlays in 2001 (in millions of dollars)
Department of Energy	
Clean Coal Technology	75
Energy Conservation Programs[h]	568
Energy Information Administration	74
Energy Supply Research and Development	655
Fossil Energy Research and Development	418
General Science and Research Activities[i]	2,993
Power Marketing Administrations	234
Department of Housing and Urban Development	
Community Development Block Grants[j]	5,058
Department of the Interior	
Bureau of Reclamation[k]	959
Bureau of Indian Affairs	2,146
Department of Transportation	
Commercial Space Transportation	12
Essential Air Service	50
Grants-in-Aid for Airports	2,174
Federal Highway Administration	
Demonstration Projects	296
Intelligent Transportation System	257
Federal Maritime Administration	
Guaranteed Loan Subsidies	93
Ocean Freight Differential Subsidies	80
Operating-Differential Subsidies	27
Federal Railroad Administration	
Amtrak Subsidies	554
Next Generation High-Speed Rail	26
Northeast Corridor Improvement Program	18
Railroad Research and Development	26
Independent Agency, Multiagency, and Other Programs	
Appalachian Regional Commission	115
Corporation for Public Broadcasting	342
Export-Import Bank	1,695
CIA: In-Q-Tel[l]	28
NASA: Aerospace Technology and Commercialization	1,369

(*continued on next page*)

(*Table A-3 continued*)

Program	Outlays in 2001 (in millions of dollars)
Overseas Private Investment Corporation	55
Partnership for a New Generation of Vehicles	298
Small Business Administration	757
Small Business Innovation Research Programs	1,000
TOTAL	**62,810**

SOURCE: Slivinski (2001).

a. The program that pays farmers not to grow crops.

b. Administers the programs of the Commodity Credit Corporation, an array of subsidies.

c. Provides subsidized loans to foreign purchasers of U.S. agricultural commodities.

d. Provides pesticide-spraying services to large private landowners and planning assistance to private forestry companies.

e. Provides subsidies, grants, and technical support to private landowners.

f. Provides grants for extension centers to assist manufacturing firms in making use of advanced manufacturing techniques.

g. The Corps of Engineers has a kernel of genuine public good in its mission—maintaining the nation's internal waterways—and a thick husk of projects that are favors for influential congressman and subsidies to hydroelectric power producers. I have assigned half of the Corps of Engineers' outlays to transfers, a conservative estimate.

h. Funds applied research to discover technologies for enhancing energy efficiency.

i. Basic research, but with such direct commercial relevance to existing high-tech industry that it qualifies as a transfer.

j. The biggest single pork barrel, with the beneficiaries divided among businesses, nonprofits, and favored towns and cities.

k. Chiefly exists to provide a subsidized water supply for agriculture in the western United States.

l. Unclassified grant program to high-tech industry for information technology projects.

The programs in table A-3 are all federal. As I stated in chapter 2, I have not tried to compile estimates of the amounts spent by states and cities on transfers to industry, nonprofits, and favored groups, but they are substantial. Cases such as municipal financing for stadiums that pad the profits of sports franchises are only the most public examples of the use of tax dollars at the state and local levels to benefit privileged groups. The annual budgets of such transfers probably add up to over $100 billion, perhaps far more, but establishing an accurate estimate would require a detailed examination of budgets around the country.

Appendix B

Computation of Budget Projections

This appendix lays out the assumptions and choices that underpin the discussion of the Plan's affordability in chapter 2. The first half of the appendix discusses how much the current system can be expected to cost in the next fifteen years; the second half turns to the computation of the projected costs of the Plan. All figures are stated in constant 2002 dollars.

Projected Costs of the Programs to Be Eliminated

Social Security and other retirement and disability programs. Projections for Social Security (more specifically, the old age, survivors, and disability insurance program, or OASDI) shown in figure B-1 are taken from the Congressional Budget Office's *The Outlook for Social Security*, released in June 2004, with the dollar figures computed by combining the data in

140

the report's figure 1-1, which shows outlays as a percentage of the gross domestic product, with the CBO's projections of GDP. The data for these calculations are contained in the "Supplemental Data" file.

Note that with OASDI (as with Medicare to come), the relevant datum is outlays, not outlays minus offsetting receipts, because total government revenues, including inflows now used to offset OASDI outlays, are part of the pool of money used to finance the Plan. Figure B-1 below shows the actual expenditures for 1980–2003 and the projected CBO numbers from 2004 to 2020. Actual expenditures are taken from U.S. Office of Management and Budget (2003).The same rate of increase was projected for the other retirement programs shown in appendix A.

FIGURE B-1
ACTUAL AND PROJECTED SOCIAL SECURITY

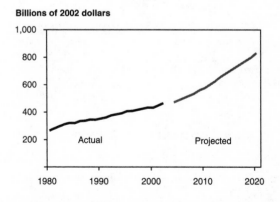

SOURCE: Congressional Budget Office (2004b).

Medicare. Actual expenditures for Medicare from 1980 to 2002 in figure B-2 below are taken from U.S. Office of Management and Budget (2003), table 3.2, line item 571. Projections for 2004–14 are taken from the CBO's September 2004 release for its periodic report, *The Budget and Economic Outlook: An Update* (hereafter *Outlook*). I have extended the estimates through 2020 using a linear extrapolation of the trendline from 2004–14—an underestimate, since the projected increases until 2014 are nonlinear.

FIGURE B-2
ACTUAL AND PROJECTED MEDICARE

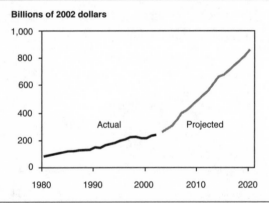

SOURCE: U.S. Office of Management and Budget (2003), U.S. Congressional Budget Office (2004a).

Unemployment compensation. Unemployment compensation is dependent on the state of the economy. There is no evidence in the data from 1980 to 2002 that the cost in constant dollars was higher during recent downturns than in earlier ones. So while the CBO projection in *Outlook* assumes that unemployment compensation will run at $40 billion to $50 billion through most of the next decade, I will assume normal economic fluctuations and apply the mean annual cost from 1980 to 2002, $25 billion per year.

Workers' compensation. In calculating expenditures, I counted premiums and benefits paid by the federal and state governments, excluding those paid by private carriers and self-insurers. In the 1990s, total annual workers' compensation costs from all sources continued to rise modestly in real terms, but the proportion paid directly from government funds dropped from a peak of about $30 billion in 1993–94 to about $20 billion since 1996. I assume that the stabilized expenditure continues, and use an unchanged cost of $20 billion from 2003 to 2020.

Transfers for persons with limited income. The dots in figure B-3 show the actual expenditures from 1980 to 2002 on the package of programs included in the Census Bureau's calculation of "Cash and Noncash Benefits for Persons with Limited Income" (table 524 in the 2005 edition of *Statistical Abstract of the United States* and comparable tables from earlier editions). The black line shows the best fit for a linear extrapolation of the experience from 1980 to 2002, while the gray line shows the best fit for a nonlinear extrapolation. The nonlinear extrapolation is the more plausible of the two—the compound annual growth rate from 1980 to 2002 was 3.8 percent. But applying the principle of optimistic projections for the current system, I use a linear extrapolation in the computations.[1]

FIGURE B-3

**ACTUAL AND PROJECTED BENEFITS FOR
PERSONS WITH LIMITED INCOME**

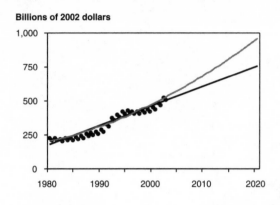

SOURCE: U.S. Bureau of the Census (2005b), table 524, and comparable tables in earlier editions

Transfers to industry, nonprofits, and favored groups.
Appendix A listed the programs classified under this heading, which added up to outlays of $62.8 billion in spending during 2001 (table A-3). Tracking the time-series spending of specific programs that make up the list in table A-3 was often not feasible because of the many additions, deletions, and changes in such programs over the years. Instead, I used table 3.2 of the U.S. Office of Management and Budget (2003), "Outlays by Function and Subfunction: 1962–2009," to identify categories of spending that are heavily weighted toward transfers to industry, nonprofits, and favored groups. The line items used for the categories are given in the note.[2] These outlays were converted to constant 2002 dollars, and

then into trend lines for 1980–2005, using 1980 as the baseline. Figure B-4 shows the results of that exercise.

FIGURE B-4

**SPENDING TRENDS FOR CATEGORIES RELEVANT
TO GROUP TRANSFERS**

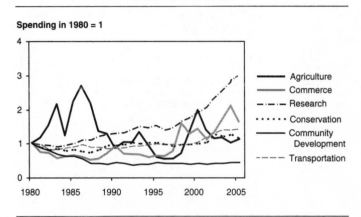

SOURCE: U.S. Office of Management and Budget (2003), table 3.2.

The experience from 1980 to 2005 is inconsistent across categories. The biggest single source of such expenditures—agriculture—has risen and fallen erratically, but spending was little higher in the early 2000s than it was in 1980. Community development expenditures fell in the 1980s and have been stable thereafter. Conservation, transportation, and commerce are modestly higher than their 1980s levels. Only the federal research budget shows a clearly rising trend, a steep one during the last eight years, but I have not been able to estimate how much of that increase has been in applied research. For purposes of projecting future costs, I have carried to an extreme the principle of being optimistic when estimating future costs of the current system, assuming that expenditures on transfers to industry, nonprofits, and favored groups will remain constant through 2020 at $63 billion.

Estimating the Cost of the Plan

The cost of the Plan depends on the average net amount received by eligible citizens, which in turn depends on income distribution, which in turn is affected by the age distribution. To estimate the costs of the Plan across the years, the following procedure was followed:

1. The Census Bureau's detailed age projections for 2000–2050, in U.S. Bureau of the Census (2004b), were used to determine the size of cohorts by age and sex for 2000–2020. The age groupings were twenty-one to thirty-four, thirty-five to forty-four, forty-five to fifty-four, fifty-five to sixty-four, and sixty-five and over.

2. U.S. Bureau of the Census (2005b), table 677, "Money Income of People—Selected Characteristics by Income Level: 2002," was used to determine the income distribution for each age/sex cell. Those data were used to estimate the average net grant for persons falling within each cell.

3. These averages were then applied to the comparable population groupings for 2000–2020.

To illustrate how the process works, consider the example of women ages thirty-five to forty-four. Using the 2002 income distribution, the percentages of all women ages thirty-five to forty-four (not just women with income[3]) who fell into various income categories were computed. This revealed that 58.1 percent of women in this age group had earned incomes of zero to $24,999. All of those women would get the full grant. In the same age group, 14.9 percent made $25,000 to $34,999, and are assumed to average $9,000 as their net grant, while 13.9 percent made $35,000 to $49,000 and are assumed to get an average of $7,000 as their net grant. A total of 13.1 percent made $50,000 or more and would get $5,000 as their net grant. Using these parameters, and multiplying the average grant by the percentages in each income category, it can be determined that, overall, women ages thirty-five to forty-four would average $8,779 as their net grant. This figure is then applied to the changing number of women ages thirty-five to forty-four over the period 2005–2020, and similarly for all age groups and both sexes. Thus, the projected costs of the Plan take into account changes in both the sex and age composition of the population, using the conservative assumption that the income distribution as of 2002 will not change.

Appendix C

Tax Rates and After-Tax Income under the Current System and the Plan

The reimbursement schedule presented in chapter 1 and the discussion of work disincentives in chapter 7 allude to the effects of the Plan on net income. This appendix shows how the tradeoffs in tax rates and after-tax income play out for different income levels under the current system and the Plan. The calculation of the payroll tax treats the entire Social Security and Medicare tax as a cost to the employee. The calculation of income tax uses the standard Internal Revenue schedules as of 2005 and assumes that the taxpayer has no deductions.

Figure C-1 summarizes the comparative tax rates all the way from $0 through $100,000 of earned income for a single person. The trend lines are unrealistic insofar as they assume zero deductions. On the other hand, the Plan does not eliminate any deductions, so the effect of

FIGURE C-1

**FEDERAL TAXES AS A PERCENTAGE OF TOTAL INCOME
UNDER THE CURRENT SYSTEM AND THE PLAN: SINGLE PERSONS**

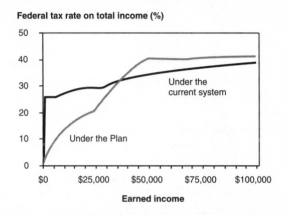

SOURCE: Author's analysis.

incorporating average deductions at each income level would shift both lines.

The first notable feature of figure C-1 is the jump from 0 to 25 percent that occurs with the first dollar of earned income under the current system. The Plan dramatically cuts the effective marginal tax rate for persons with earned income of less than $36,000. All with incomes over $36,000 who file as single taxpayers have a higher tax rate under the Plan than they do now (though their net incomes are nonetheless higher because of the grant). The maximum percentage increase is faced by single people making $49,000 a year, and amounts to 6.1 percentage points above their current rate.

Why not stretch the reimbursement schedule over a broader income range so that more of it is paid by higher-income families? Two considerations led me to stay with $50,000. The first is that the effects of the Plan on married couples with one income are much different than the effects on single persons, as figure C-2 shows.

FIGURE C-2
FEDERAL TAXES AS A PERCENTAGE OF TOTAL INCOME UNDER THE CURRENT SYSTEM AND THE PLAN: MARRIED COUPLES WITH ONE INCOME

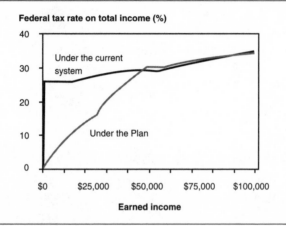

SOURCE: Author's analysis.

The large reduction in effective tax rate for low-income families remains, but now the reduction extends through families with $46,000 in earned income. For families above that point, the effective tax rate under the Plan is nearly identical to the one they pay now (and the rates could easily be made identical without importantly affecting tax revenues). This contrast between the tax hike facing single persons with incomes above $36,000 and the lack of a tax hike facing married couples with one income may rightly be interpreted as favoring one-income marriages. It is a feature of the Plan that I deem to be one of its merits, for reasons discussed in chapter 10.

The second consideration is that a focus on tax rates tends to obscure the state of affairs regarding actual tax payments. Thus the arguments against proposals for a flat tax tend to ignore that an affluent person who makes ten times as much money as a poor person pays ten times as much money in taxes, even though their rates are identical. Similarly, even though people in the $36,000–$50,000 range take a modestly harder hit in tax rates than those making more than $50,000, the tax reimbursement schedule for the Plan nonetheless gives them larger real-dollar increases in income than it gives more affluent persons. Figure C-3 on the following page shows after-tax income from $0 through $100,000 in earned income. For this graph, I return to the case of the single taxpayer. The trend lines for married couples with one income have the same relative position before and after the Plan goes into effect.

Annual after-tax income is higher across the income range, and proportionally higher in the same income range that incurs the greater increase in effective tax rate. The question remains whether the increased annual income during the working years enjoyed by people making higher incomes is worth the loss of Social Security and Medicare benefits. That is the topic of appendix D.

Table C-1 shows the tax rates and after-tax income for each $1,000 increment in income from $25,000 to $50,000,

FIGURE C-3

**AFTER-TAX INCOME UNDER THE CURRENT SYSTEM
AND THE PLAN: SINGLE PERSONS**

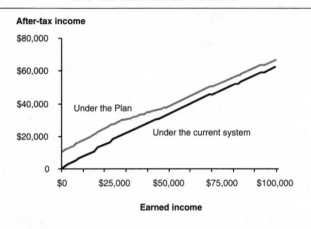

SOURCE: Author's analysis.

the range over which the surtax on the grant applies, for single taxpayers. Table C-2 replicates that information for married couples with one income filing jointly. The calculations treat the entire grant as income, even though $3,000 is earmarked for health care. To obtain after-tax cash income, simply subtract $3,000 from the figures in the far right-hand column.

TABLE C-1
TAXES AND AFTER-TAX INCOME FOR SINGLE PERSONS

Total income		Taxes			Tax rate on total income		After-tax income	
Current system	The Plan	Payroll (15.3%)	Income tax single person	Surtax on the grant	Current system	The Plan	Current system	The Plan
$25,000	$34,800	$3,825	$3,400	$0	28.9%	20.6%	$17,775	$27,775
$26,000	$35,600	$3,978	$3,550	$200	29.0%	21.6%	$18,472	$28,272
$27,000	$36,400	$4,131	$3,700	$400	29.0%	22.5%	$19,169	$28,769
$28,000	$37,200	$4,284	$3,850	$600	29.1%	23.4%	$19,866	$29,266
$29,000	$38,000	$4,437	$4,060	$800	29.3%	24.3%	$20,503	$29,703
$30,000	$38,800	$4,590	$4,310	$1,000	29.7%	25.4%	$21,100	$30,100
$31,000	$39,600	$4,743	$4,560	$1,200	30.0%	26.4%	$21,697	$30,497
$32,000	$40,400	$4,896	$4,810	$1,400	30.3%	27.4%	$22,294	$30,894
$33,000	$41,200	$5,049	$5,060	$1,600	30.6%	28.3%	$22,891	$31,291
$34,000	$42,000	$5,202	$5,310	$1,800	30.9%	29.2%	$23,488	$31,688
$35,000	$42,800	$5,355	$5,560	$2,000	31.2%	30.0%	$24,085	$32,085
$36,000	$43,600	$5,508	$5,810	$2,200	31.4%	30.9%	$24,682	$32,482

(continued on next page)

(*Table C-1 continued*)

Total income		Taxes			Tax rate on total income		After-tax income	
Current system	The Plan	Payroll (15.3%)	Income tax single person	Surtax on the grant	Current system	The Plan	Current system	The Plan
$37,000	$44,400	$5,661	$6,060	$2,400	31.7%	31.7%	$25,279	$32,879
$38,000	$45,200	$5,814	$6,310	$2,600	31.9%	32.4%	$25,876	$33,276
$39,000	$46,000	$5,967	$6,560	$2,800	32.1%	33.2%	$26,473	$33,673
$40,000	$46,800	$6,120	$6,810	$3,000	32.3%	33.9%	$27,070	$34,070
$41,000	$47,600	$6,273	$7,060	$3,200	32.5%	34.6%	$27,667	$34,467
$42,000	$48,400	$6,426	$7,310	$3,400	32.7%	35.3%	$28,264	$34,864
$43,000	$49,200	$6,579	$7,560	$3,600	32.9%	35.9%	$28,861	$35,261
$44,000	$50,000	$6,732	$7,810	$3,800	33.1%	36.5%	$29,458	$35,658
$45,000	$50,800	$6,885	$8,060	$4,000	33.2%	37.1%	$30,055	$35,055
$46,000	$51,600	$7,038	$8,310	$4,200	33.4%	37.7%	$30,652	$36,452
$47,000	$52,400	$7,191	$8,560	$4,400	33.5%	38.3%	$31,249	$36,849
$48,000	$53,200	$7,344	$8,810	$4,600	33.7%	38.9%	$31,846	$37,246
$49,000	$54,000	$7,497	$9,060	$4,800	33.8%	39.4%	$32,443	$37,643
$50,000	$55,000	$7,650	$9,310	$5,000	33.9%	39.9%	$33,040	$38,040

SOURCE: Author's analysis.

TABLE C-2
TAXES AND AFTER-TAX INCOME FOR MARRIED COUPLES WITH ONE INCOME

Total income		Taxes			Tax rate on total income		After-tax income	
Current system	The Plan	Payroll (15.3%)	Income tax married couple	Surtax on the grant	Current system	The Plan	Current system	The Plan
$25,000	$44,800	$3,825	$3,050	$0	27.5%	15.3%	$18,125	$38,125
$26,000	$45,600	$3,978	$3,200	$200	27.6%	16.1%	$18,822	$38,622
$27,000	$46,400	$4,131	$3,350	$400	27.7%	16.9%	$19,519	$39,119
$28,000	$47,200	$4,284	$3,500	$600	27.8%	17.7%	$20,216	$39,616
$29,000	$48,000	$4,437	$3,650	$800	27.9%	18.4%	$20,913	$40,113
$30,000	$48,800	$4,590	$3,800	$1,000	28.0%	19.2%	$21,610	$40,610
$31,000	$49,600	$4,743	$3,950	$1,200	28.0%	19.9%	$22,307	$41,107
$32,000	$50,400	$4,896	$4,100	$1,400	28.1%	20.5%	$23,004	$41,604
$33,000	$51,200	$5,049	$4,250	$1,600	28.2%	21.2%	$23,701	$42,101
$34,000	$52,000	$5,202	$4,400	$1,800	28.2%	21.8%	$24,398	$42,598
$35,000	$52,800	$5,355	$4,550	$2,000	28.3%	22.5%	$25,095	$43,095
$36,000	$53,600	$5,508	$4,700	$2,200	28.4%	23.1%	$25,792	$43,592

(continued on next page)

(Table C-2 continued)

Total income		Taxes			Tax rate on total income		After-tax income	
Current system	The Plan	Payroll (15.3%)	Income tax married couple	Surtax on the grant	Current system	The Plan	Current system	The Plan
$37,000	$54,400	$5,661	$4,850	$2,400	28.4%	23.6%	$26,489	$44,089
$38,000	$55,200	$5,814	$5,000	$2,600	28.5%	24.2%	$27,186	$44,586
$39,000	$56,000	$5,967	$5,150	$2,800	28.5%	24.8%	$27,883	$45,083
$40,000	$56,800	$6,120	$5,300	$3,000	28.6%	25.3%	$28,580	$45,580
$41,000	$57,600	$6,273	$5,450	$3,200	28.6%	25.8%	$29,277	$46,077
$42,000	$58,400	$6,426	$5,600	$3,400	28.6%	26.3%	$29,974	$46,574
$43,000	$59,200	$6,579	$5,750	$3,600	28.7%	26.8%	$30,671	$47,071
$44,000	$60,000	$6,732	$5,900	$3,800	28.7%	27.3%	$31,368	$47,568
$45,000	$60,800	$6,885	$6,050	$4,000	28.7%	27.8%	$32,065	$48,065
$46,000	$61,600	$7,038	$6,200	$4,200	28.8%	28.2%	$32,762	$48,562
$47,000	$62,400	$7,191	$6,350	$4,400	28.8%	28.7%	$33,459	$49,059
$48,000	$63,200	$7,344	$6,500	$4,600	28.8%	29.1%	$34,156	$49,556
$49,000	$64,000	$7,497	$6,650	$4,800	28.9%	29.5%	$34,853	$50,053
$50,000	$65,000	$7,650	$6,800	$5,000	28.9%	29.9%	$35,550	$50,550

SOURCE: Author's analysis.

Appendix D

Preliminary Thoughts about Political Feasibility and Transition Costs

This appendix addresses the question of political feasibility of the Plan, with particular reference to the people in midlife who would have to accept the transition from the current system to the Plan. By *political feasibility* I do not mean whether Congress can be persuaded to pass the Plan, but whether it is in the self-interest of a broad majority of Americans. Imagine that somehow the Plan were put to a referendum in which individual Americans were asked to vote it up or down. Does the Plan ask a large proportion of the electorate to vote against its own best interests?

The comparison between the current system and the Plan for low-income Americans was discussed in chapters 3 and 5. The Plan is less generous than the current system for all single mothers under twenty-one and for some single mothers over twenty-one who do not work. For everyone else below the income median who comes into the Plan as a young person, the Plan offers a much better deal than the current system.

The issue of political feasibility centers on upper-income taxpayers and those who are in midlife at the time the transition to the Plan occurs. The obvious reason that people who make more money might rationally prefer the current system is that the amount of money that they put into Social Security and Medicare is greater than the net they get from the grant. As of 2005, an employee and employer are each taxed an amount equal to 6.2 percent of the employee's salary for FICA and another 1.45 percent each for Medicare. The current income cap for FICA is $90,000. Medicare has no income cap. For a person making $90,000, the direct cost is thus $6,885. Since the employer's contribution to Social Security and Medicare is coming out of the pool of money available to pay wages, the real contributions are twice those amounts, but even without adding in the employer's contribution, all people making more than $65,360 are putting more into the current system than the $5,000 they will take out of the Plan.

Furthermore, the Plan does not offer them the carrot of being freed from FICA and Medicare taxes, because the financial feasibility of the Plan is based on the assumption that total government revenues will be the same as they would be under the current system. There is no way to reconfigure the tax system so that middle-income and affluent citizens do not end up paying just about as much tax as they do now. The first question thus becomes what benefits they are giving up under the current system, and the second question is how much they would get back under the Plan.

The Forgone Benefits from the Current System for the Middle Class and Above

A person or family switching from the current system to the Plan gives up prospective Social Security benefits and Medicare. In calculating their value, I assume that the promised benefits of the current system will actually be there when the time comes—a generous assumption.

In this appendix, we are considering people who will pay close to the maximum FICA taxes throughout their careers. Such twenty-one-year-olds just entering the system are looking at the prospect of about $25,000 a year from Social Security when they retire.

The dollar value of the Medicare benefit depends on personal utility functions that will vary from person to person. As a benchmark, I use Medicare disbursements per enrollee per year. In 2002, that figure was about $6,400. I will add a fudge factor, taking $7,000 in cash as the current indifference point between having the Medicare benefit and having more income.[1]

Adding Social Security and Medicare, middle-income and affluent Americans thus stand to get about $32,000 per year in benefits from the current system when they retire. To assess whether they should rationally support the Plan, I consider first the case of young people who would spend

WHAT DO THE AFFLUENT NEED
THE GOVERNMENT FOR?

What other government benefits besides Medicare and Social Security do those in the upper half of America's income distribution give up under the Plan?

The number that loses major benefits is small. Eliminating corporate welfare will affect the bottom line of the corporations that are getting sweetheart deals, but it will not produce massive layoffs of executives across America. The affluent will no longer have unemployment insurance, but the prospective loss of unemployment insurance is not important to many of them or, for that matter, to many people who have graduated from college. (An exercise for readers: Ask your friends with college degrees if they have ever gotten unemployment payments and, of those, how many actually needed them.)

In terms of social justice, the cuts in the programs that benefit the affluent involve few of the moral considerations posed by cuts in programs for the poor. Farmers (affluent or not) will lose agricultural subsidies.[2] They should. Corporations that have benefited from government favoritism will lose income. They should. East Coast commuters will have to pay the market price for railway service when Amtrak is gone. They should. In all of these cases, some citizens are now being given private benefits denied to other Americans..

Socially just or not, here is the larger truth: If government existed exclusively of national defense, police services, the courts, and public goods such as sewers

(continued on next page)

(continued from previous page)

and highways, the vast majority of people in the upper half of the American income distribution would get along just fine. Most of their experience with government does not involve benefits, but unwanted encounters with the IRS, regulatory agencies, and their state's Motor Vehicle Administration.

---

their entire lives under the Plan, and then turn to those who would be caught in the transition from the current system to the Plan.

Young People Who Would Spend Their Working Lives under the Plan and Who Expect Soon to Be Making More than $50,000 a Year

A large proportion of young adults about to turn twenty-one, including just about everyone who is in college, expects to be making more than $50,000 fairly soon in their careers. Why should they support the Plan?

The answer exposes how inefficient the current system is: Even while paying in more than the $5,000 the government gives back, they can expect to be better off under the Plan when the time comes to retire. To illustrate, take someone who graduates from college at twenty-one and immediately gets a job paying more than $50,000 a year, and therefore never gets more than the $5,000 minimum. He spends the average $3,000 on health care, leaving just $2,000 from the grant, which he invests annually in a retirement account that returns the standard 4 percent I have been assuming. When he retires at age sixty-seven, he will have $253,741, a sum that will purchase an annuity of about $21,000. If he were to have no other retirement income, his net retirement package replacing Social Security would thus bring in $28,000 net (assuming a continuing $3,000 annually for health care)—about $3,000 more than he would get from Social Security under the current system. If he had $50,000 annually in private retirement income, his package from the Plan would consist of continuing health care plus $23,000. For practical purposes, the current system and the Plan are about equivalent.

But that's not the end of a sensible young person's calculations. Four percent is a minimal return. Hardly any of these same young people who expect to be making more than $50,000 would think it realistic to assume that they will get so little from their stock portfolio over the long term. And they're right. Recall the discussion in chapter 3: If you invest your money in a fund indexed to the stock market for forty-five years and get only a 4 percent return, you will have gotten less than you would have gotten from any forty-five year period in the history of the United States since 1801.

Suppose that our young man gets the average, a 7 percent annual real return over that forty-five years. In that case, his accumulation will be $613,504, purchasing an annuity worth about $51,000 per year. Add in the continuing grant, and the net advantage of the Plan under this scenario is between $28,000 and $33,000 in retirement income per year. So, as our twenty-one-year-old looks to the future, the Plan promises benefits no worse than the current system, if he is extremely unlucky, and a big bonus if he lives in a merely average era.

So far, I am assuming that our young man will remain single all his life. If instead he marries, the prospective benefits of the Plan for him and his wife double if she works full time at a similarly remunerative job, and far more than double if she becomes a full-time mother (because she generates a substantial retirement income of her own that would not have existed at all under the current system).

The bottom line: If we are talking about a twenty-one-year-old choosing between the current system or the Plan, even those who expect to become affluent get a better deal under the Plan.

Let me take this to an extreme. Suppose we have a twenty-one-year-old who says to himself, "I'm really stupid with money. I won't save any. I'll make bad investments. I will reach retirement with nothing but my $10,000 a year. Therefore I prefer to stick with the current system." He is not being rational. If he is able to think that about himself in that way at age twenty-one, the rational next step is to say, "Therefore I will sign an irrevocable contract that commits $2,000 from my annual grant, divided among several conservative investment firms, for investment in index-based portfolios." The only way that the current system could be *rationally* preferred by an affluent twenty-one-year-old is if he could expect the next forty-five years to be economically the worst in American history and that, in spite of this, the current system could continue to make good on its obligations—an impossible combination. I have said it before in this book, but it bears repeating and italicizing: *The current system cannot meet its obligations if the American economy does not continue to grow at a rate that would produce the private returns assumed by the Plan.*

People Older than Twenty-One

What is true for a twenty-one-year-old is not necessarily true for a forty- or fifty-year-old. Under what circumstances does the Plan offer a worse deal than the current system? If the Plan were actually to be implemented, some provision must be made for those who have played by the current system's rules with specific expectations about the current system's payoffs.

To calculate a technically defensible estimate of transition costs from the current system to the Plan would take a team of economists months of work. It involves some extremely complex modeling and the acquisition of detailed economic and demographic data on a wide variety of issues. For our purposes, I start with the assumption that if the annual savings under the Plan after 2011 are anywhere close to my estimates as shown in chapter 2, there has to be a way to pay for the transition. The differential in cost between the current system and the Plan in the out-years is too huge for the answer to be otherwise. But, in the short term, the transition costs would be huge as well. I am not trivializing the problem of transition, but making a simpler point: If we wanted to switch to the Plan badly enough, we could do it. Strategies are available for coping with the one-time transition costs. Here, I will offer a few specific examples in support of that proposition.

Affluent households paying the maximum surtax. In thinking about what would be required to make the Plan acceptable to people who would lose money from it, I will start with the specific example of a couple who are both age fifty and stand to lose the most in benefits from the current system by switching to the Plan. They both work, and have been earning the maximum Social Security wage base all of their working lives. For calculating the size of their net grant after they retire, I assume that each will have private pension incomes so large that they will get a net grant of only $5,000 each after retirement.

For couples in midlife when the Plan begins, I dispense with the assumption that they are required to spend $3,000 per year for medical care, and assign Medicare an annual value of $7,000 per person (see p. 159). Table D-1 summarizes their situations under the current system and if they were to enter the Plan at fifty, assuming that they invest the entire amount of the grant and get an average real return of 4 percent.

This couple can expect a grand total of $58,700 a year in benefits from the current system. If each of them starts contributing $5,000 annually to a retirement fund to replace

TABLE D-1

TRADEOFF BETWEEN THE RETIREMENT BENEFITS OF THE
CURRENT SYSTEM AND THE PLAN FOR AN AFFLUENT TWO-INCOME
COUPLE ENTERING THE PLAN AT AGE FIFTY

Source of combined annual income	Under the current system	Under the Plan
Social Security	$44,700	0
Value of Medicare	$14,000	0
Annuity from the accumulated grant	0	$17,200
Continuing cash grant	0	$10,000
TOTAL	$58,700	$27,200

SOURCE: Author's analysis.

this income, by age sixty-six they will each have accumulated $109,123, enough to buy annuities totaling about $17,200 in annual income. They will lose about $31,500 a year by switching to the Plan.

How much would the government have to give this couple to make up the difference? In the case shown in the table, the severance payment must be enough to buy annuities generating $31,500 a year, starting in sixteen years. To do that, the government would have to give the couple about $214,000 right now.

It sounds expensive. Actually, it is not much different from the cost of letting the couple remain on the current system. At age fifty, the average person can expect to live for another 30.3 years (more if a woman, less if a man; I'll simplify and use the average).[3] Thus, the government can expect to pay the couple $44,700 per year in Social Security benefits for about fourteen years (starting at age sixty-six) and $14,000 in Medicare benefits per year for fifteen years (starting at sixty-five)—a total nominal obligation of about $836,000.[4] Those obligations must be discounted. Using the standard assumption of a 4 percent real return, the present value of a $44,000 payment twenty-five years from now is only $16,505. Applying this logic to all the payments, the present value of the government's obligations to this fifty-year-old couple is about $370,000.

Suppose instead that the couple is put on the Plan. This means we can expect to pay them a combined total of $10,000 per year for thirty years ($5,000 each, assuming that they are at the maximum surtax on the grant throughout retirement as well as during their working years). This nominal cost of $300,000 works out to a present value of about $183,000. To that, we must also add the cost of some subsidy that makes up any difference between the current cost of the couple's health insurance and its cost after the Plan goes into effect for the rest of their working lives (see the note for a discussion of this).[5] I cannot estimate that figure precisely, but suppose it is somewhere from $1,000 and $3,000 per person per year for a couple aged fifty. This implies that the present value of the government's prospective obligations under the Plan ranges from $208,000 to $259,000. Both of these numbers are substantially less than the $370,000 owed under the current system.

This does not point straight to a policy for handling the transition. I specified that both spouses continued to work full-time, making high salaries, from age fifty to sixty-six.

One of them might have planned to retire at fifty-one any-way, greatly increasing the advantages of joining the Plan even without a severance payment. For now, the point is merely that the government's obligations to that fifty-year-old couple are so great under the current system that it can afford to offer a large severance payment.

Furthermore, this encouraging arithmetic continues even for those close to retirement. For a two-income, affluent cou-ple who are both age sixty, for example, the present value of the obligations of the current system is about $634,000, while the present value of the obligations under the Plan would be in the range of $192,000 to $229,00, giving the government over $400,000 to use for a severance package that the affluent couple would prefer to the current system.[6]

Now reconsider that same couple at age fifty—same total household income, same household private retirement income—with just one difference: This has always been a one-income household; the wife has never worked outside the home, and she will therefore get no Social Security, knocking $22,350 off the couple's retirement income under the current system.[7] The Plan specifies that someone with-out income gets the full grant, no matter what the spouse makes. Thus, instead of getting a net grant of $10,000 a year, the affluent one-income family gets $15,000. Table D-2 shows the changed tradeoffs.

The expected value of the benefits under the Plan exceed those under the current system by $5,200 before incorporat-ing the required amount of insurance subsidy. After incorpo-rating it, deficit is somewhere between $20,000 and $70,000.

TABLE D-2

TRADEOFF BETWEEN THE RETIREMENT BENEFITS OF THE CURRENT
SYSTEM AND THE PLAN FOR AN AFFLUENT ONE-INCOME COUPLE
ENTERING THE PLAN AT AGE FIFTY

Source of combined annual income	Under the current system	Under the Plan
Social Security	$22,350	0
Value of Medicare	$14,000	0
Combined annuities from the accumulated grant	0	$26,200
Continuing cash grant	0	$15,000
TOTAL	$36,350	$41,200

SOURCE: Author's analysis.

Middle-income households paying the maximum surtax.
The patterns that apply to the affluent couple generalize to all
households with incomes of $50,000 or above. To establish
the lower end of the range, consider a person age fifty with
an income barely at the maximum surtax level of $50,000.
This person has not paid the maximum rate to Social Security
all his life, and thus has smaller benefits than the affluent
household. For purposes of calculating the surtax on his
post-retirement grant, I will assume that he has a private pension that will pay him $25,000 after retirement. Assume two
scenarios: (1) his spouse has never worked outside the home
and has no pension, and (2) his spouse also makes $50,000
with the same prospective pension. Table D-3 shows the result
before incorporating the medical insurance subsidy.

TABLE D-3

TRADEOFF BETWEEN THE RETIREMENT BENEFITS OF THE CURRENT
SYSTEM AND THE PLAN FOR A PERSON MAKING $50,000 AND
ENTERING THE PLAN AT AGE FIFTY

Household and income combination	Prospective government benefits under ...		Present value of the government's obligation under ...	
	the current system	the Plan	the current system	the Plan
Spouse has never worked outside the home	$27,800	$43,876	$179,401	$295,371
Spouse also makes $50,000, has same pension	$41,600	$33,960	$164,600	$224,900

SOURCE: Author's analysis.

For one-income couples, even after adjusting for a medical subsidy, switching to the Plan is preferable (and continues to be so well into their fifties). For two-income couples, a modest subsidy would be required at age fifty, but one that is much less than the present value of the government's obligations under current system.

The permutations are numerous—spouses who once worked and have now stopped working, one spouse with a large salary and another with a small one—all of which produce different results. But the specific value of the severance payment that would produce equivalence in retirement incomes is not as important as the larger point: For one-income couples, the Plan is always preferable for anyone younger than their mid-fifties. For two-income couples, the present value of a one-time severance payment is manageable even under the assumptions I have been using.

Having said that, I will point out that those assumptions are conservative. The actual size of the severance payment needed to induce large proportions of older taxpayers to leave the current system would be smaller than I have presented.

To see why, return to the example of the two-income affluent couple who have paid the maximum Social Security contribution all their lives. To make it easier to follow the comparisons, I ignore the medical subsidy in these calculations (assumed earlier to run from $1,000 to $3,000 per year per person). That amount, whatever it turns out to be, is a constant added to the debit side of the Plan.

In the initial calculations for that couple, I concluded that the severance payment needed for equivalence was $214,000 before the medical subsidy. But I based that on the assumption of a 4 percent return and an annual Medicare value of $7,000. For an affluent couple, neither of those assumptions applies. After retirement, they will spend whatever they want to spend, on whatever physicians they prefer, regardless of what Medicare does or doesn't cover. The real value they get from Medicare is nowhere near its value for someone who depends exclusively on Medicare. And none of their assumptions about money management assumes a 4 percent return. On both counts, their calculations of their own best interests will differ from the ones I have used.

Suppose, for example, that they value Medicare at only $3,500 a year and expect a 7 percent return on their money. In that case, the severance payment at age fifty that would produce the same retirement benefits under the Plan as under the current system would be not $214,000, but just $87,000.

With retirement only sixteen years away, they might not want to shift to the Plan for that payment because of the greater volatility of investment returns for shorter time horizons. Some sweetener might have to be offered to make the switch attractive—but the government would have lots of negotiating room. To continue with the running example: Using the 4 percent assumption, the present value of the government's obligations to the affluent two-income couple is $370,000 for the current system and $187,000 under the Plan. In other words, the government would save $183,000 if the couple were shifted to the Plan.

Suppose it offers 75 percent of that amount, or about $137,000, to the affluent couple. The affluent couple looks at that amount and asks what accumulation they will have by the time they retire. If they get a 7 percent return, it will be $404,000. On top of that, they will have each been receiving $5,000 annually from the cash grant, which they expect to accumulate to about $279,000 by the time they turn sixty-six. With the combined total, they can purchase an annuity worth about $54,000 a year, compared to the $44,700 they will get under Social Security— and they will continue to receive another $10,000 a year ($5,000 each) after retirement. It is an extremely attractive deal, despite the uncertainties of rate of return over a sixteen-year period. Even after giving them the severance grant, the government will be spending less on this couple than they would have spent under the current system.

I opened the appendix by asking whether middle-income and affluent Americans would be voting their personal interests if they supported the Plan. For the overwhelming majority of them, the answer is yes. The Plan offers a better deal to all such persons into their mid-thirties, and to some very large proportion of them into their fifties if they live as a couple in a one-income household. The only group that would require a substantial incentive to make the Plan preferable to the current system consists of couples in which both husband and wife are past their mid-thirties, both make more than $50,000, and both plan to continue working until retirement age.

In considering transition costs, I have argued that even within the relatively small segment of the population that would rationally prefer to remain in the current system, all but those on the verge of actually retiring could be bought off with a lump-sum payment that represents less than the present value of the government's obligations to those couples under the current system. Nothing in this perspective denies that the transition costs would be large and problematic. But neither should we stop considering the Plan because the prospective transition costs are obviously unmanageable.

Appendix E

Assumptions about the Costs of the Current System versus the Costs of the Plan

In chapter 2, I proposed to err on the high side when projecting the costs of the Plan and to err on the low side when calculating and projecting the costs of the current system. In this appendix I list all the specific instances in which the principle has been applied.

1. Estimates of the cost of the Plan use Census Bureau estimates and projections of the resident population ages twenty-one and older, which assumes that all residents are citizens and eligible for the grant, consisting as of 2002 of at least seven million more people than the actual number who would be eligible for the grant.

2. Estimates of the cost of the current system do not include any of the costs of retirement for government

employees, even though their pension systems often fold Social Security into their benefit package without calling it Social Security.

3. The designation of programs for the category "Corporations, Groups, and Favored Individuals" excludes many programs that could reasonably be classified under that heading.

4. Estimates of the costs of the current system exclude many state, county, and municipal transfer programs. Revenue estimates to pay for the Plan do not include the taxes used to pay for those programs.

5. The costs of the current system are based on benefit payments, ignoring many billions of dollars in administrative costs.

6. The projected cost of the Plan assumes no change in the income distribution, even though historical experience indicates that the percentage of people paying the maximum surtax will continue to increase.

7. Future costs of means-tested transfer programs (Medicaid, food stamps, TANF, and so on) assume a linear increase, even though past experience indicates that nonlinear increases are more likely.

8. Costs of Medicare from 2014 to 2020 are assumed to be linear, even though the CBO projections from 2004 to 2014 increase nonlinearly.

9. The annual cost of unemployment compensation from 2005 to 2020 is assumed to equal the mean

176 IN OUR HANDS

cost from 1980 to 2002, less than half of the average
annual cost projected by the CBO.

10. The calculations of accumulations in retirement
accounts under the Plan assume an average of a
4 percent real return, more conservative than the
assumptions used by the Social Security Administration or the CBO in projecting real returns from
the stock market, and lower than the average return
from any forty-five-year period since 1801. Historically, the average annual real return from the
stock market has been 7 percent.

Notes

Introduction

1. The long version is Murray (1988). The short version is Murray (1997).

PART I

Chapter 1: The Plan

1. The article was Stigler (1946). Stigler revealed that the idea came from Friedman in later correspondence. Burkhauser and Finegan (1993), 128.

2. Friedman (1962), 191–94.

3. Lampman (1965).

4. For a summary of the results of the NIT experiment, see Murray (1984), chapter 11.

5. The official poverty rate is what gets the publicity every year, and it has remained effectively unchanged since the 1970s. The official measure has failed to capture many aspects of poverty that have declined, and equally, does not capture indicators revealing that the size of the underclass has increased. See Eberstadt (2005) for the former argument and Murray (1999) for the latter. Whether a good measure of quality of life among people in the bottom income

quintile would have gone up or down since the 1970s depends on how one weights outcomes such as increased car ownership among poor people versus increased family breakdown among poor people.

6. If so desired, the amount of the grant could be adjusted monthly, based on income-to-date in that calendar year, with a year-end adjustment to correct for over- or underpayments because of unusual fluctuations in income.

7. If this option were used, the definition of median earned income would have to be based on the median for the entire population age twenty-one and over, not the median for people with income, so that changes in labor force participation would be reflected in lowered median income.

8. Services that are required for the operation of the courts and criminal justice system are also retained. For example, the enforcement of child-abuse laws sometimes means that children must be taken from their parents. Doing so requires that the local government (for this would be an instance of a local responsibility) provide for the well-being of that child through whatever facilities and services might be chosen by that locality

Chapter 2: Basic Finances

1. U.S. Bureau of the Census (2004b). The major publications of the Census Bureau are now available online, and subsequent citations of those publications will refer to their web versions.

2. I am assuming that convicted criminals do not get the grant while they are incarcerated, but resume their eligibility when they are released or paroled. I estimate the number of incarcerated people ages twenty-one and over at about 1.7 million, based on Bureau of Justice Statistics figures showing a little over 2 million persons in prisons and jails as of 2002, and surveys of the age distribution of prisoners. U.S. Department of Justice, Office of Justice Programs, Bureau of Justice Statistics (2005). Estimating the number of noncitizens is problematic because estimates of the illegal immigrant population are guesswork, but the number cannot be smaller than 5 million. See U.S. Bureau of the Census (2005b), tables 2, 6, and 7.

3. U.S. Bureau of the Census (2005b), table 677.

4. This estimate is based on the distribution of incomes in the $25,000 to $50,000 range by sex and age as of 2002, and the tax

schedule described in the note above. See appendix B for a description of the procedure. The actual amount would be affected by the progressivity of the surtax and changes in the income distribution within the $25,000 to $50,000 range. (The year after the Plan is implemented, the number of jobs paying $45,000 to $49,999 would diminish drastically, with new concentrations of jobs in the low forties and low fifties.)

5. U.S. Bureau of the Census (2005b), table 677.

6. Ibid., table 524.

7. Ibid., table 519.

8. The actual totals for these programs were obtained from the 2001 outlays (Slivinski 2001), and amounted to $62.81 billion, which I rounded to $63 billion for 2002 outlays. For reasons explained in appendix B, I decided to assume $63 billion as a constant spending level for these programs in calculating the projected costs of the current system.

9. Reaching an exact figure would require a major research project of its own. The most recent data for state and local expenditures as I write are for 2001. U.S. Bureau of the Census (2005b), table 428, shows a total of $418.8 billion spent by state and local governments on public welfare, health and hospitals, and housing and community development. An indeterminate portion of this duplicates expenditures I classify under the means-tested programs, which includes $134.0 billion of state and local expenditures (table 524). Table 428 also shows state and local revenue from the federal government at $204.2 billion for public welfare, health and hospitals, and housing and community development. An indeterminate portion of this may duplicate expenditures reported under the federal portion of means-tested expenditures in table 524. Thus, the costs of the separate state and local programs in these categories range from a minimum of $80.6 billion to a maximum of $418.8 billion. To complicate matters further, many transfers by state and local governments are hidden within categories such as highways, natural resources, and parks and recreation, which total $157.3 billion, and in the $194.6 billion of the direct general expenditure total that is not broken out by category.

10. I have not discussed administrative expenses because they are trivial. The Plan is just about as simple as a program can be. To administer it, the government needs to know when every United States citizen is born and dies and, after age twenty-one, the number of a bank

account into which money can be deposited. State governments already keep birth and death records. The Plan adds to these existing records a stipulation that a universal passport be issued at birth. Given this setup, the Plan could be administered using a computerized payment system plus a capability for investigating fraud—by government standards, a tiny agency. The Social Security Administration (SSA) reports that it spends less than 1 percent of its budget on administrative costs. Disregarding whether the SSA is run efficiently, administering Social Security is far more complex than administering the Plan. The SSA must issue Social Security cards, keep track of contributions over the years, and keep track of survivors.

In any case, the administrative costs make no difference to the Plan's feasibility, because the sums of money involved are so huge. Even if they amounted to 1 percent, annual administrative costs would be about $20 billion—a trivial amount compared to the total budget. But that number is nonetheless far too large. An estimate of $5 billion, mostly devoted to investigation of fraud, would be closer. One of the most satisfying aesthetic aspects of the Plan is how little money can be siphoned off to support bureaucracies.

It should also be noted that most of the administrative expenses of the current system are not captured in the data used to estimate its cost, because the reported data consistently are framed in terms of benefits paid, not total costs. An accurate figure for the real administrative costs of the current system would add tens of billions of dollars to the estimates I present—another instance in which the figures presented here consistently understate the costs of the current system.

11. The aging of the population will increase the cost of the Plan because, on average, people over age sixty-five will pay back less of the grant than people under sixty-five.

12. The precise estimate is 1.03 percent for the period 2005–2020. Whenever I refer to an average rate of increase, I mean the compound average growth rate (CAGR), not the arithmetic average.

13. See appendix B for data sources and methods. If the time period chosen were 1990–2000, the corresponding CAGR would be 3.1 percent. If the time period were 1970–2000, it would be 4.5 percent. My use of the 2.9 percent CAGR from 1980–2000 is a conservative basis for stating the historical cost increases of the programs to be replaced. The same statement applies if

per-capita increases in real costs are used instead of total increases in real costs.

14. The computations and sources are found in appendix B.

15. U.S. Department of Labor, Bureau of Labor Statistics, and U.S. Bureau of the Census (2004).

16. The time series comes from U.S. Bureau of the Census (2005a), table P-54.

17. I use men for the example because median female income rose steadily throughout the entire period 1970–2001.

18. The percentage of people in the $25,000 to $50,000 range stays about the same—a growing number of people move into that range over time, but a growing number also move up and out. In 1970–2000, 26.3 percent of persons with incomes made $25,000 to $49,999 (in 2001 dollars). In 2001, that figure was 27.5 percent (U.S. Bureau of the Census [2005a], table P-54). This point is elaborated in appendix B.

19. The assumption that the income distribution stays the same is not only an upper bound; it is based on the assumption that the economy does not expand from now to 2020. In either of those cases, the current system would be bankrupt, and comparisons of costs are meaningless.

PART II
Chapter 3: Retirement

1. In 2002, the poverty rates were 10.4 percent for people ages sixty-five and older versus 12.1 percent overall. U.S. Bureau of the Census (2004a), tables 2 and 5.

2. Ibid., table 5.

3. For example, a woman who got her first job at fifty in 1988 for $9,500 a year and stayed there until sixty-five, when it paid $20,000, is getting $7,452 a year in Social Security benefits. The calculation was done online using the tools available through the U.S. Social Security Administration (2004), applying the benefit levels as of October 2005.

4. I specified that the person was born in 1983, began earning $20,000 in 2001, and will continue earning $20,000 through retirement.

5. U.S. Bureau of the Census (2004a), p. 4.

6. This is the first of many times that I will discuss cumulative contributions by retirement age. The problem is that the government's definition of the standard retirement age moves from 66 to 67 in the years to come. I will sometimes (as in this case) be talking about younger workers for whom the standard retirement age is 67 and at other times (e.g., in appendix D) about people for whom that age is 66. Shifting my frame of reference accordingly seems needlessly confusing. I have chosen to refer uniformly to a forty-five-year period from age 21 to retirement.

7. This figure combines the employer's and employee's contribution.

8. Calculated at ImmediateAnnuities.com (1996–2005), using Maryland as the state (a typical state), and using the values that applied as of spring, 2005. I am not suggesting that buying an annuity would be the best use of the accumulated money. It is simply a conservative way of comparing retirement income under the Plan with the annuity provided by Social Security.

9. U.S. Social Security Administration (2002); U.S. Congressional Budget Office (2003).

10. These and the following figures are taken from Siegel (1998), chapter 1, updated through 2001, as posted on Siegel's website.

11. As always, the average represents the compound annual growth rate (CAGR), not an arithmetic average.

12. The long-term consistency of returns of this magnitude is not limited to the United States. Siegel goes on to demonstrate that over the period 1926–97, spanning the Great Depression and World War II, the compound average real return for Germany, the United Kingdom, and Japan, all of which saw their economies ruined in the 1940s, were 6.6 percent, 6.2 percent, and 4.3 percent, respectively. It should also be noted that Japan's average return is measured in dollars, understating the increase in purchasing power that the Japanese enjoyed (the yen substantially appreciated against the dollar over that period). Siegel (1998), 19.

13. In the next chapter, I will amend the Plan to require everyone to spend $3,000 of the grant on health care every year, meaning that the above examples need to be amended to $7,000, $14,000, and $42,000 in cash resources, adding in the value of health insurance they have been required to obtain.

14. U.S. Congressional Budget Office (2003).

15. The joint relationship of IQ to socioeconomic status and personality traits such as judgment, impulsivity, and substance abuse is sufficiently strong to lead to this expectation. For reviews of the literature on IQ's relationship to these variables, see Herrnstein and Murray, 1994.

16. Note that year-to-year volatility in the stock market is not an issue for retirement funds. The question is worst cases when money is put into the stock market and left for extended periods.

Chapter 4: Health Care

1. Until well into the twentieth century, the things that medicine could do to extend life and improve quality of life were limited to a few surgical operations, a few inoculations, and medications that mainly alleviated symptoms. Improved nutrition and the prevention of disease through sanitation were the main reasons for increasing lifespans during the early decades of the century. The commercial production of antibiotics was one landmark change in this situation. Another was a rapid expansion in surgical capabilities. But these developments didn't gain momentum until the 1930s.

2. "MinuteClinic," currently operating in the Minneapolis and Baltimore areas, is an example of the kind of operation I have in mind, though the MinuteClinic facilities, located in places such as Target Drug stores, are more limited in their services than I envision. They are unable to operate in most jurisdictions because of regulation. Even if they were freed of regulation, their popularity would be limited as long as the actual out-of-pocket cost of a visit to a MinuteClinic and to one's personal physician remained the same, as it does for millions of people with employer-provided insurance.

3. Center to Advance Palliative Care (2002).

4. U.S. Department of Labor, Bureau of Labor Statistics (2005), table 2-7.

5. This doesn't mean that a person could opt for a highly restricted policy A at age twenty-one and at age fifty switch over to a more comprehensive policy B without paying the difference (plus compound interest) between his inflation-adjusted aggregate premiums for A and what he would have paid for B if he had enrolled in it at twenty-one, nor does it mean that insurance companies cannot change the

price of insurance policies in accordance with changes in health-care costs. The policy I propose means that the rate that people are paying for a policy already in place is the same for all ages in any given year.

6. This is another instance in which health care is *sui generis*. People at age twenty-one also have radically different abilities to, say, become astrophysicists, for reasons completely beyond their control. If it is appropriate to use the state to compensate for the random inequality that makes some people likely to get muscular dystrophy, why not use the state to compensate for other random inequalities by aggressively pursuing equality in material condition of all kinds? The difference between the two kinds of innate inequality is this: I may not have the capacity to become an astrophysicist, but that says nothing about what I want out of life. The goods I choose to maximize might be income, quality of family life, leisure, or a dozen others, depending on my preferences. The idea that someone will automatically want to be equal to everyone else in material condition does not fit with what we know about ourselves and other humans. In contrast, everyone who faces the prospect of a serious health problem wants the good called medical care.

7. The single-pool rule will also transform the health insurance market. Every insurance company must figure out rates it can live with when it must accept any applicant, and every insurance company knows that every other insurance company is faced with the same calculus. Thus, every insurance company would prefer to put all of its agencies in places where people are likely to be healthy (for example, affluent neighborhoods) and none of its agencies in places where people are likely to be unhealthy (such as poor neighborhoods), but they won't be able to get away with it. Everyone, including people from poor neighborhoods, is going to be in the insurance market, and every insurance company is required to sell to them. The most likely result of a single-pool rule is that the insurance industry establishes a national risk pool for allocating unprofitable customers. But it might not work out that way. Many smart and motivated people will be figuring out new ways to make a profit in a single-pool world, and forecasting what entrepreneurs will come up with when faced with a new market worth hundreds of billions of dollars is impossible.

8. Over the long term, this statement is true for a population in which fertility is at replacement level or above. In a population that is

rapidly getting older, the costs of caring for a growing elderly population will increase the average premium for everyone—already a serious problem in Europe; still a minor problem in the United States, where the population is aging, but fertility is still at the replacement level.

9. I am indebted to Wilson Taylor, former CEO of Cigna Corporation, for obtaining these calculations. The numbers assume a continuation of the current system and projected increases in health-care costs over the next forty-five years. In practice, few if any companies would literally write a forty-five-year policy because of what is known in the insurance business as *ruin theory*. The company would be required to make too many assumptions, any one of which, if wrong, would mean bankruptcy twenty or thirty years down the road. But a person presenting himself to an insurance company ready to make a long-term commitment as a twenty-one-year-old is an extremely attractive customer. The figures represent the current best estimate of what it would take to make a profit, and hence the nature of the deal it would offer to induce these attractive customers to sign up. As in other comparisons between the Plan and the current system, an objection that applies to that conclusion applies to the current system as well. If ruinous inflation hits the Plan, ruinous inflation will also have hit the current system. If breakthroughs in technology mean that the coverage couldn't be comprehensive, the same breakthroughs will have strained the current system.

10. U.S. Bureau of the Census (2005b), tables 126 and 127.

11. A side effect of eliminating the tax exclusion for employer-paid health insurance would be to increase tax revenues by about $145 billion in 2004, according to a CBO study, U.S. Congressional Budget Office (2005), available at http://www.cbo.gov/showdoc .cfm?index=6075andsequence=19. But one of my ground rules is that the Plan be revenue-neutral, so I do not include this extra revenue in the discussion of its affordability.

Those who worry that this will lead to lower wages (employers drop the medical benefits but don't increase pay) are reminded that a job is worth a certain amount of money, whether paid in cash or in cash plus benefits. Take away the health benefits, and the company cannot keep the same quality of employees without correspondingly increasing the cash. In a reverse way, this kind of calculation originally led employers to become providers of medical benefits. When wages were frozen during World War II, employers found they could bypass the wage freeze and attract employees by offering medical benefits. It's all about compensation, regardless of the form.

12. Readers who have faith in state licensing laws should take a look at how that licensing is actually done. The degree hanging on a physician's wall is a much more reliable indicator of the quality of the physician's training than the state's rubber stamp, and certification by a physician-run professional association is a much more rigorous test of competence. In a world where medical technicians were permitted to provide routine medical care without operating under the direct supervision of a physician, similar profession-generated signals of training and competence would inevitably be created—as they always are, in every skilled profession, when the government does not intervene.

13. For a general history of tort law and malpractice, see Studdert et al. (2004). For specifics on physicians withdrawing services, see Brooks et al. (2004).

14. Kessler and McClellan (1996).

Chapter 5: Poverty

1. This and the following poverty thresholds are taken from U.S. Bureau of the Census (2004a).

2. The precise amounts are $20,712 annually for a man and $19,704 for a woman. For the computation of annuities, I used the calculator at ImmediateAnnuities.com.

3. U.S. Bureau of the Census (2005b), table 620. The official label for this job category is "cleaning and building service."

4. The official poverty line was developed in 1963 by a task force from the Social Security Administration headed by Molly Orshansky. It was based on the finding that food took about a third of the average family's budget. The original poverty line consisted of three times the cost of adequate nutrition, varying by family size. The definition was subject to many criticisms even at the time, but that initial set of numbers still forms the basis for today's poverty line, adjusted for the cost of living.

The official poverty line is hopelessly outmoded, bearing hardly any relationship either to poverty or to a family's total resources. For example, in deciding whether a family is under the poverty line, the value of food stamps, Medicaid, and public housing assistance, programs which were enacted after the poverty definition was created, are ignored. In deciding whether a cohabiting person is under the poverty line, only the individual's income is counted—a woman with no income living with a man making $30,000 a year is counted as poor. These defects alone make the poverty line uninterpretable as a real measure of poverty, but they are compounded by another problem: underreporting of income. The Bureau of Labor Statistics' annual Consumer Expenditure Survey consistently finds that people in the bottom income quintile spend twice as much as they report making. U.S. Department of Labor, Bureau of Labor Statistics (2003).

5. U.S. Bureau of the Census (2003), table 3, combining median earnings of full-time, year-round male and female workers. The Bureau of the Census defines full-time, year-round workers as people who worked fifty or more weeks and 35 or more hours per week—in other words, at least 1,750 hours per year.

6. For estimating the value of the EITC under varying conditions, I used the EITC Estimator at the website of the Center for Budget Policy and Priorities; Center for Budget Policy and Priorities (2005). For estimating TANF payments by state, I used the state-by-state information on the website of the National Center for Children in Poverty (2003). For estimating food stamp payments, I used the calculators on the websites of Food USA and the U.S. Department of Agriculture, Food and Nutrition Service.

Chapter 6: The Underclass

1. For an explanation of the importance of these three indicators, see Murray (1999).

2. The poor commit more crimes than the not-poor, but the rate at which they commit crime has increased internationally over a century in which both the extent of poverty and its severity fell. More sophisticated analyses have shown a relationship between unemployment and crime, but a small and inconsistent one. For reviews of the literature, see Freeman (1999) and Piehl (1998).

3. Martin, Hamilton, and Sutton, et al. (2005), table 17.

4. A widespread misconception about the welfare reform of 1996 is that it got rid of welfare. It put new initials on the cash grant (TANF instead of AFDC) and made it harder to keep getting the cash grant indefinitely, but had no important effect on the short-term economic realities facing a teenage girl who gets pregnant.

5. Anderson (1993)

6. Sullivan (1993).

7. I would argue that more adoptions of babies born to single young women would be a good outcome for the children, however painful for the mothers. Adoption is by no means a cure-all, however. Studies of adopted children have found that intellectual and personality development is determined primarily by the characteristics of the birth parents, with the adoptive environment playing a lesser role (for example, van IJzendoorn et al. [2005], Rhee and Waldman [2002]). But adoption has a good track record for providing nurturing, healthy environments for children, and young unmarried mothers do not. Two basic sources of evidence on these issues are Bartholet (1999) and McLanahan and Sandefur (1994). Whether increased abortions among single young women is good or bad depends primarily on personal views that are beyond the reach of data. For those who consider abortion to be equivalent to murder, empirical issues are irrelevant. Others should note that John Donohue and Steven Levitt have argued that abortion explains part of the reduction in crime. The validity of this finding remains hotly debated. A recent defense of the Donohue/Levitt position is Levitt (2004).

8. This figure refers to an average state, not the high-benefit state of California for which figures were presented in chapter 5. For someone receiving the average TANF grant and the maximum food stamp allotment for a family of two, the cash-like annual income from the current system as of 2002 was $8,300. Average monthly TANF assistance per family in 2002 was $418.30. U.S. Department of Health and Human Services, Administration for Children and Families, Office of Family Assistance, *TANF Annual Report* to *Congress* (2004), table 1:14. The food stamp allotment for a family of two with no income is $274 per month. U.S. Department of Agriculture, Food and Nutrition Service (2004). Add in Medicaid plus benefits that may be received through housing assistance, the school breakfast and lunch programs, the WIC (women, infants, and

children) program, child- and adult-care food program, housing assistance, Head Start, TANF services, child care for TANF recipients, and low-income energy assistance, and the value of a typical package for a woman who does not work easily surpasses $10,000. For women who work, the TANF and food stamp grants are reduced, but other programs kick in, with the earned income tax credit being the most important.

9. The one way that this sure bet could fail is if the Plan were to reduce the number of marriages. There is no reason to expect that it would, for reasons described in chapter 10.

10. For a systematic statement of why I conclude that births to unmarried women drive the formation and growth of the underclass, and how the absence of males behaving as responsible fathers contributes, see Murray (1994).

11. The trend lines for labor force participation by age and race from 1954–1980 are shown in Murray (1984), 77.

12. Unpublished tabulations from the Current Population Survey provided courtesy of the Bureau of Labor Statistics.

13. Shaw (1916), act V.

Chapter 7: Work Disincentives

1. Again assuming that retirement contributions are voluntary. Under Plan B, the cash gross would be $29,999.

2. The top marginal rate for total taxes (not just the grant) reaches 60 percent at $30,000 of earned income and stays there until $50,000 of earned income. If the question is whether a marginal rate that high will have any work disincentive effects, the answer is surely yes. But in thinking about the prospective magnitude of the effect, it is useful to see how this marginal rate looks from ground level. Consider a single man earning $34,000 a year who, under the Plan as I have presented it, has an after-tax cash income of $28,688. This figure has deducted the $3,000 for health care. "After tax" refers to federal taxes; I am ignoring state and local taxes for this calculation. He gets a raise to $35,000, at which point he has an after-tax income of $29,085. The difference is $397, meaning that he is paying a 60.3 percent marginal tax rate on the extra thousand dollars of income. This seems far too severe, so let us say that somehow the Plan can be constructed so that he is

paying the marginal rate for existing federal taxes, but no marginal taxes on the grant. His total after-tax income for that year would be increased by only $200. That represents an increase of seven-tenths of one percent of his after-tax income over the amount he pays under the Plan as I have presented it. It would be interesting to know how many people keep track of their after-tax income to within less a percentage point of the total, but I cannot imagine that it is a large number. Meanwhile, there is another and more straightforward way of looking at the marginal tax, and that many people will be aware of: Of the extra $1,000 of earned income between $34,000 and $35,000, the surtax takes only $200. See appendix C for a detailed presentation of tax rates and after-tax income at different levels of income.

3. Another advantage of the Plan is that it gives no added incentive to work off the books for any job paying less than $25,000. The incentive that exists now—to keep the IRS in the dark—will continue, but the Plan adds nothing new. Even if the government finds out that someone is working off the books, it will have no effect on the size of his grant. The Plan increases the incentive to work off the books only for jobs that pay more than $25,000, and few off-the-book jobs pay that well.

4. For the eighteen to twenty-one age group, 44.5 percent were neither in high school nor in college. U.S. Bureau of the Census (2005b), table 256.

5. In 2001, the average earnings of year-round, full-time workers ages eighteen to twenty-four with a high school diploma were $23,416 for men and $19,902 for women. Ibid., table 695.

6. My urgings to my children to delay graduate school after college have worked so far; my urgings to delay entering college went unheeded by the first three children but may work with the fourth.

PART III

Chapter 8: The Pursuit of Happiness in Advanced Societies

1. For an example of how two people can look at the same continent and come away with diametrically opposed conclusions, compare this discussion of the Europe Syndrome with Jeremy Rifkin's

The European Dream: How Europe's Vision of the Future is Quietly Eclipsing the American Dream. Rifkin (2004).

2. U.S. Bureau of the Census (2005b), tables 70 and 1327.

3. The replacement level is 2.1 births per woman—the Total Fertility Rate, or TFR. As of 2003, the TFRs for France, Germany, Italy, the Netherlands, Spain, and the United Kingdom, even after incorporating the high rates of their recent non-European immigrants, were just 1.9, 1.4, 1.3, 1.7, 1.3, and 1.7, respectively. Take out the effects of the immigrant births, and the TFRs for the native populations of those countries are in the region of half the replacement rate. In the United States, the TFR in 2003 was 2.1. Ibid., table 1325.

4. To clarify the role of wealth: One's material situation is not irrelevant to happiness (people who lived through the Great Depression were likely forever after to name financial security as something they were consciously grateful for), but neither is it central. Severe financial worries can impede happiness, but once financial worries are minor, the opposite of financial worries—wealth—is seldom a source of active happiness. Wealth can provide any variety of momentary pleasures, but "money can't buy happiness" seems to be true. Or at least I have never met anyone with much money who tried to dispute it.

5. Walzer (1983), 278–79.

6. Some readers will have realized that my raw materials for pursuing happiness consist of Abraham Maslow's Needs Hierarchy, and are wondering what else I have borrowed from other thinkers. You can find a detailed presentation of these arguments, along with scholarly attribution of their origins, in a book I wrote many years ago entitled *In Pursuit: Of Happiness and Good Government* (1988).

7. In this formulation, I fold the institutions of faith into the institution I call *community*.

8. Richard J. Herrnstein formulated the *matching law*, a mathematical expression of the way in which people pursue their interests without maximizing them. See Herrnstein (1997).

9. For a discussion of the ways in which the findings of modern social science inform the question of whether humans have a moral sense, see Wilson (1993).

10. Smith ([1759] 1979). See especially Part III, "Of the Foundation of our Judgments concerning our own Sentiments and Conduct, and of the Sense of Duty."

11. John Adams, *Discourses on Davila* (1790), quoted in Lovejoy (1961), 190–91.

Chapter 10: Marriage

1. For people in the middle of the range from "responsible" to "irresponsible," the distribution of effects will be mixed. The availability of a guaranteed income will surely tip the scales toward marriage for some couples who would be better off not marrying, but equally tip others toward marriage who, once married, will make a success of it. In netting out the effect of the Plan on the decision to marry, I assume no bad effects among the most irresponsible, roughly fifty-fifty effects among those in the middle of the continuum, and unambiguously positive effects among the most responsible. Those who want to make the case that the net effect will be negative have to assume that, under the current system, most of those who are deterred from marriage by economic considerations are toward the irresponsible end of the continuum—an argument which, to me, is a contradiction in terms.

2. In some states, under some circumstances, an unmarried biological father could be held responsible for the child, but they were exceptional.

3. The evaluation of the NIT experiments in the 1970s initially found negative effects on marriage (Murray 1984). Since then, the reality of those effects has been the subject of dispute (Cain and Wissoker 1990, Hannan and Tuma 1990). But this debate is as irrelevant to the Plan as the findings about the NIT experiment's work disincentives, and for the same reason: The NIT experiment temporarily provided a low income floor on top of existing transfers, while the Plan permanently replaces all transfer programs with a large income supplement. The incentives generated by the two programs are radically different.

4. The literature discussing the negative effects of being raised by a cohabiting or never-married mother on the well-being of children is large and growing. Surveys that convey the nature of the findings and also have references to additional literature are McLanahan (1999) and Popenoe (1999).

5. I acknowledge a complication: What is best for the children? The technical literature suggests that, *ceteris paribus*, a full-time

mother at home is preferable to a mother who works outside the home, as common sense leads one to expect. But it is not clear from that literature what happens if the results are disaggregated into children whose mothers are at work because they want to be and children whose mothers are at home because they have to be. Children do best in happy marriages. Marriages are less likely to be happy when the woman is being a full-time mother when she doesn't want to be. I do not know how this trades off with the advantages of having a full-time mother, even a reluctant one.

6. With an income of $50,000, the man has a net of $5,000 from the grant, with $3,000 of that going to health care, or a net of $52,000 in cash. The woman has $7,000 in cash from the grant, for a family cash income of $59,000. Note that I have chosen a comparison with the current system which implicitly assumes that the husband's job currently provides medical coverage for both him and his wife. If that were not the case, and the woman under the current system were paying for her own medical coverage, then the Plan has a much more powerful effect on enabling her to stay at home full time.

7. I say *mothers* because that's who will stay home under the Plan, overwhelmingly. There's no point in saying *parents* and conveying the impression that it will be a toss-up whether the father or mother decides to be a stay-at-home parent. But of course my argument applies to fathers as well.

Chapter 11: Community

1. Tocqueville ([1835] 1969), 513.

2. Ibid., 515, 517.

3. For data and discussion of the shift from membership groups to advocacy groups, see Skocpol (2003), 127–74.

4. For data on the timing and magnitude of the decline of the fraternal associations, see Skocpol (2003), 90–91.

5. In the latter part of the nineteenth century, for example, the highest ratio of Odd Fellows lodges per 100,000 population was found among northern blacks. Skocpol (2003), 55. In combination with black churches, the fraternal organizations constituted the social backbone of black communities that were far healthier in their family structure and social norms than are today's inner cities. For a

classic account of the role of these institutions see DuBois ([1899] 1967), chapter 12. For an account of the black family before the welfare state, see Gutman (1976).

6. Beito (2002), 197.

7. Skocpol (2003), 90.

8. Quoted in Beito (2002), 182, citing New Hampshire Bureau of Labor, *Report* (1894).

9. Olasky (1992), 86.

10. Pollock (1923), in Skocpol (2003), 63–64.

11. In 2002 dollars, the average annual earnings in 1900 for all occupations was about $9,500; in nonfarm occupations, about $10,600 (U.S. Bureau of the Census [1975]: D779–D793), which typically had to support a family with at least two children, usually more. The poverty threshold for a family of four in 2002 was $18,244.

12. Riis (1890), chapter 16, para. 7.

13. See for example Skocpol (2003), Beito (2000), and Olasky (1992).

14. The story is told about a researcher in the 1980s who was comparing New York City's Roman Catholic parochial schools with the New York City public school system. After he had assembled data on the size of the mammoth administrative staff of the public schools, he phoned the head office of the parochial schools, only to be told by the voice on the other end of the phone that they did not keep information on the number of administrative staff. The researcher persisted. Finally, the voice said, "All right. Wait a minute and I'll count." I have forgotten the name of the researcher, and cannot guarantee that the story is not apocryphal, but it accurately conveys the difference in the bureaucratic superstructure in public and private schools.

15. Burke (1791).

16. The role of voluntary associations in fostering virtue was direct and powerful, as Theda Skocpol has described, even in an age when racial and gender segregation were taken for granted. "[M]embership associations may often have restricted membership," she writes, ". . . but every category of the population combined into similarly organized cross-class federations expressing much the same Judeo-Christian and patriotic worldviews. Ironically, this had the effect of pulling American citizens together—teaching them shared

values and similar citizenship practices—even when they did not intend to be united" Skocpol (2003), 117.

APPENDIXES

Appendix A

1. Slivinski (2001).

Appendix B

1. The CBO does not give a projection for the package of programs included in the table "Cash and Noncash Benefits for Persons with Limited Income." It does give projections for several of the specific programs included in this category: supplemental security income, EITC, food stamps, family support (welfare), child nutrition, and social services. The difficulty in accepting these projections is that they are constrained to fit existing provisions in the law. Thus, for example, table 1-4 in *Outlook* shows the earned income and child tax credits as remaining roughly constant at $42 billion to $44 billion through 2011, then dropping to $32 billion in 2012–14. If Congress does nothing to change the law, this sudden drop in projected EITC might be reasonable. But it is not reasonable to expect that Congress will permit a sudden funding decrease for one of the most popular income support programs.

The result of the CBO's assumptions about the stability of current legislative provisions leads it to project increases in costs for these programs for the eleven years from 2003 to 2014 at 19 percent, about a third as large the *lowest* observed real increase in the cost of the package of programs for low-income persons—58 percent— over any eleven-year period from 1980–91 to 1991–2002. The average increase over that set of eleven-year periods is 70 percent. In this instance, application of the principle of optimism in computing the costs of the current system is served by striking a middle ground. The linear extrapolation I use for the projections works out to a 30 percent gross increase in the costs of the programs over the next eleven years, about half of the lowest eleven-year increase we have observed since 1980.

2. The line items, numbered as in the *Historical Tables* (U.S. Office of Management and Budget [2003], table 3.2), are as follows:

Agriculture: 351 Farm income stabilization and 352 Agricultural research and services.

Conservation: 301 Water resources and 302 Conservation and land management.

Commerce: 376 Other advancement of commerce.

Transportation: 401 Ground transportation, 402 Air transportation, 403 Water transportation, 407 Other transportation.

Community development: 451 Community development and 452 Area and regional development.

Research: 251 General science and basic research and 552 Health research and training.

3. When reporting median earned income, the Bureau of Labor Statistics routinely bases the median on the population of people with incomes. But since the Plan deals with all persons ages twenty-one and over, the relevant statistic is the median based on all persons within a given age and sex category, not just persons with income.

Appendix D

1. That figure will rise substantially in the future, but, as in all cases, analyzing today's tradeoffs can be extrapolated to the future. Suppose Medicare benefits skyrocket. In one sense, $7,000 wouldn't be enough to compensate for the loss of Medicare. In another sense, the same scenario makes the eventual demise of Medicare much more likely, and having $7,000 in cash instead becomes increasingly attractive.

2. I don't count farmers among the affluent, though many with enough land to receive large subsidies are. Affluent or not, the number of farmers who lose subsidies they cannot replace by substituting other crops constitutes only a portion of farmers, and all farmers combined constitute just 1 percent of American workers.

3. All figures on life expectancy are taken from Arias (2004).

4. As noted earlier, the average cost of Medicare per enrollee in 2002 was about $6,400. If I were to use this number, which makes

the current system cheaper than the $7,000 I have been using as the value of Medicare, then I should go back and recalculate the comparison of the current system versus the Plan using $6,400—which would make the Plan look even more attractive. In this discussion, the key is to keep using the same assumptions throughout.

5. One of the problems of the transition that is too complex to take up in detail involves medical insurance for those in midlife. Our hypothetical couple is in the upper middle class and have been taking care of their own health insurance. Here's one scenario out of many that illustrates the possibilities. Let's say that the husband and wife each have employer-provided insurance. The Plan goes into effect, whereupon their employers drop their coverage, giving everyone the per-employee cost of the insurance as a wage increase. If insurance companies are to able to sell this fifty-year-old couple individual insurance at the standard rates (constant throughout the age span) that I discussed in chapter 4, how much subsidy will they need, over and above the amount that the couple was already paying? Whether that amount is a lot or a little is not at all obvious (remember that many new insurance buyers of ages twenty-two, twenty-three, etc., will also be entering the insurance market). But some subsidy will probably be required, and the amount of that subsidy will rise along with the age of those people involved in the transition.

6. For this older couple, I assume that the subsidy for topping off their health insurance costs until retirement is somewhere between $3,000 and $6,000 annually.

7. This Social Security income is based on someone age fifty now, and is somewhat smaller than the $24,000 that a twenty-one-year-old entering the system is promised.

References

Anderson, E. 1993. Sex Codes and Family Life among Poor Inner-City Youths. In *Young Unwed Fathers: Changing Roles and Emerging Policies*, ed. R. I. Lerman and T. J. Ooms. Philadelphia: Temple University Press, 74–98.

Arias, E. 2004. United States Life Tables, 2002. *National Vital Statistics Reports* 53 (6). Available at http://www.cdc.gov/nchs/data/nvsr/nvsr53/nvsr53_06.pdf

Bartholet, E. 1999. *Nobody's Children: Abuse and Neglect, Foster Drift, and the Adoption Alternative*. Boston: Beacon Press.

Beito, D. T. 2000. *From Mutual Aid to the Welfare State: Fraternal Societies and Social Services, 1890–1967*. Chapel Hill, N.C.: University of North Carolina Press.

———. 2002. This Enormous Army. In *The Voluntary City: Choice, Community, and Civil Society*, ed. D. T. Beito, P. Gordon, and A. Tabarrok. Ann Arbor, Mich.: University of Michigan Press.

Brooks, R. G., N. Menachemi, C. Hughes, and A. Clawson. 2004. Impact of the Medical Professional Liability Insurance Crisis on Access to Care in Florida. *Archives of Internal Medicine* 164: 2217–22.

Burke, E. 1791. Letter to a Member of the National Assembly. In *The Maxims and Reflections of Burke*, ed. F. W. Rafferty, http://www.ourcivilisation.com/smartboard/shop/burkee/maxims/chap18.htm (accessed October 4, 2005).

200 IN OUR HANDS

Burkhauser, R. V., and T. A. Finegan. 1993. The Economics of Minimum Wage Legislation Revisited. *Cato Journal* 13 (1): 123–29.

Cain, G. G., and D. A. Wissoker. 1990. A Reanalysis of Marital Stability in the Seattle-Denver Income-Maintenance Experiment. *American Journal of Sociology* 95: 1235–69.

Center to Advance Palliative Care. 2002. How to Establish a Palliative Care Program: End of Life Expenditures. In *CAPC Manual*, February 20, http://64.85.16.230/educate/content/elements/expendituresforeolcare.html (accessed October 4, 2005).

Center for Budget Policy and Priorities. 2005. EITC Estimator, http://www.cbpp.org/eic2005/eitcm1.htm (accessed October 4, 2005).

DuBois, W. E. B. [1899] 1967. *The Philadelphia Negro: A Social Study.* New York: Benjamin Blom.

Eberstadt, N. 2005. Broken Yardstick. *New York Times*, September 9.

Food USA. n.d. Food stamps calculator, http://www.foodstamps.org/age.htm (accessed October 4, 2005).

Freeman, R. B. 1999. The Economics of Crime. In *Handbook of Labor Economics*, ed. O. Ashenfelter and D. Card, vol. 3. New York: Elsevier Science, 3529–71.

Friedman, M. 1962. *Capitalism and Freedom.* Chicago: University of Chicago Press.

Gutman, H. G. 1976. *The Black Family in Slavery and Freedom 1750-1925.* New York: Vintage Books.

Hannan, M. T., and N. B. Tuma. 1990. A Reassessment of the Effect of Income Maintenance on Marital Dissolution in the Seattle-Denver Experiment. *American Journal of Sociology* 95: 1270–98.

Herrnstein, R. J. 1997. *The Matching Law: Papers in Psychology and Economics.* Cambridge, Mass.: Harvard University Press.

Herrnstein, R. J., and C. Murray. 1994. *The Bell Curve: Intelligence and Class Structure in American Life.* New York: Free Press.

ImmediateAnnuities.com. 1996–2005. Annuity calculator, http://www.immediateannuities.com (accessed October 4, 2005).

Kessler, D., and M. McClellan. 1996. Do Doctors Practice Defensive Medicine? *Quarterly Journal of Economics* 111 (2): 353–90.

Lampman, R. 1965. Approaches to the Reduction of Poverty. *American Economic Review* 55:521–29.

Levitt, S. D. 2004. Understanding Why Crime Fell in the 1990s: Four Factors that Explain the Decline and Six that Do Not. *Journal of Economic Perspectives* 18 (1): 163–90.

Lovejoy, A. O. 1961. *Reflections on Human Nature*. Baltimore, Md.: Johns Hopkins University Press.

Martin, J. A., B. E. Hamilton, P. D. Sutton, et al. 2005. Births: Final Data for 2003. *National Vital Statistics Reports* 54 (2). Hyattsville, Maryland: National Center for Health Statistics.

McLanahan, S. 1999. Father Absence and the Welfare of Children. In *Coping with Divorce, Single Parenting, and Remarriage: A Risk and Resiliency Perspective*, ed. M. Hetherington. Mahwah, N.J.: Lawrence Erlbaum Associates.

McLanahan, S., and G. Sandefur. 1994. *Growing Up with a Single Parent*. Cambridge, Mass.: Harvard University Press.

Murray, C. 1984. *Losing Ground: American Social Policy 1950–1980*. New York: Basic Books.

———. 1988. *In Pursuit: Of Happiness and Good Government*. New York: Simon and Schuster.

———. 1994. What to Do about Welfare. *Commentary*. December.

———. 1997. *What It Means to Be a Libertarian*. New York: Broadway Books.

———. 1999. *The Underclass Revisited*. Washington, D.C.: AEI Press.

National Center for Children in Poverty. 2003. 50-State Data Wizards, http://nccp.org/wizard/wizard.cgi (accessed October 4, 2005).

Olasky, M. 1992. *The Tragedy of American Compassion*. Washington, D.C.: Regnery Gateway.

Piehl, A. M. 1998. Economic Conditions, Work, and Crime. In *The Handbook of Crime and Punishment*, ed. M. Tonry, 302–19. New York: Oxford University Press.

Pollock, I. L. 1923. *The Food Administration in Iowa*, vol. 1. Iowa City: State Historical Society of Iowa.

Popenoe, D. 1999. *Life Without Father: Compelling New Evidence that Fatherhood and Marriage Are Indispensable for the Good of Children and Society*. Cambridge, Mass.: Harvard University Press.

Rhee, S. H., and I. D. Waldman. 2002. Genetic and Environmental Influences On Antisocial Behavior: A Meta-Analysis Of Twin and Adoption Studies. *Psychological Bulletin* 128 (3): 490–529.

Rifkin, J. 2004. *The European Dream: How Europe's Vision of the Future is Quietly Eclipsing the American Dream*. New York: Penguin.

Riis, J. 1890. *How the Other Half Lives: Studies among the Tenements of New York*. New York: Charles Scribner's Sons. Hypertext edition available at http://www.yale.edu/amstud/inforev/riis/title.html (accessed October 4, 2005).

Shaw, G. B. 1916. *Pygmalion.* Hypertext edition available at http://drama.eserver.org/plays/modern/pygmalion/default.html (accessed March 23, 2005).

Siegel, J. 1998. *Stocks for the Long Run: The Definitive Guide to Financial Market Returns and Long-Term Investment Strategies*, 2nd ed. New York: McGraw-Hill, Updated through 2001 at http://www.jeremy siegel.com (accessed October 4, 2005).

Skocpol, T. 2003. *Diminished Democracy: From Membership to Management in American Life.* Norman, Okla.: University of Oklahoma Press.

Slivinski, S. 2001. The Corporate Welfare Budget Bigger than Ever. *Policy Analysis*, no. 415.

Smith, A. [1759] 1979. *The Theory of Moral Sentiments.* Oxford: Oxford University Press.

Stigler, G. 1946. The Economics of Minimum Wage Legislation. *American Economic Review* 36 (June): 358–65.

Studdert, D. M., M. M. Mello, and T. A. Brennan. 2004. Medical Malpractice. *New England Journal of Medicine* 350:283–92.

Sullivan, M. L. 1993. Young Fathers and Parenting in Two Inner-City Neighborhoods. In *Young Unwed Fathers: Changing Roles and Emerging Policies*, ed. R. I. Lerman and T. J. Ooms. Philadelphia: Temple University Press, 52–73.

Tocqueville, A. de. [1835] 1969. *Democracy in America.* Trans. G. Lawrence. Garden City, N.Y.: Anchor Books.

U.S. Bureau of the Census. 1975. *Historical Statistics of the United States, Colonial Times to 1970*, vol. 1. Washington, D.C.: U. S. Bureau of the Census.

———. 2003. *Income in the United States: 2002.* C. DeNavas-Walt, R. Cleveland, and B. H. Webster Jr. Current Population Reports, P60-221. Washington, D.C.: U. S. Bureau of the Census.

———. 2004a. Poverty 2002. In *Current Population Survey, 2003.* Annual social and economic supplement, http://www.census.gov/ hhes/poverty/threshld/thresh02.html (accessed October 4, 2005).

———. 2004b. Projected Population of the United States by Age and Sex: 2000–2050. Table 2a in *U.S. Interim Projections by Age, Sex, Race, and Hispanic Origin*, http://www.census.gov/ipc/www/ usinterimproj/natprojtab02a.pdf (accessed October 4, 2005).

———. 2005a. Historical Income Tables. In *Current Population Survey*. Annual social and economic supplement, http://www.census.gov/hhes/income/histinc/p54.html (accessed October 4, 2005).

———. 2005b. *Statistical Abstract of the United States 2004–2005*, http://www.census.gov/prod/www/statistical-abstract-04.html (accessed October 4, 2005).

U. S. Congressional Budget Office. 2003. *Evaluating and Accounting for Federal Investment in Corporate Stocks and Other Private Securities*. Washington, D.C.: Congress of the United States.

———. 2004a. *The Budget and Economic Outlook: An Update.* Washington, D.C.: Congress of the United States.

———. 2004b. *The Outlook for Social Security.* Washington, D.C.: Congress of the United States.

———. 2005. *Budget Options.* Washington, D.C.: Congress of the United States.

U.S. Department of Agriculture, Food and Nutrition Service. 2004. Applicants and Recipients Allotment Chart, October 6, http://www.fns.usda.gov/fsp/applicant_recipients/allotmentchart.htm (accessed October 4, 2005).

———. n.d. Food Stamps Pre-Screening Eligibility Tool, http://209.48.219. 49/fns/ (accessed October 4, 2005).

U.S. Department of Health and Human Services, Administration for Children and Families, Office of Family Assistance. 2004. *TANF Annual Report to Congress*, last updated July 10, http://www.acf.hhs.gov/programs/ofa/annualreport6/chapter01/0114.htm (accessed October 4, 2005).

U.S. Department of Justice, Office of Justice Programs, Bureau of Justice Statistics. 2005. Corrections Estimates, http://www.ojp.usdoj.gov/bjs/correct.htm (accessed October 4, 2005).

U.S. Department of Labor, Bureau of Labor Statistics. 2003. *Consumer Expenditure Survey*, http://www.bls.gov/cex (accessed October 4, 2005).

———. 2004. Bureau of Labor Statistics, and U.S. Bureau of the Census. Annual Demographic Survey. March supplement. http://ferret.bls.census.gov/macro/032003/perinc/new01_001.htm (accessed October 4, 2005).

———. 2005. *Consumer Expenditures in 2003*, report 986, June, http://www.bls.gov/cex/csxann03.pdf (accessed October 4, 2005).

U.S. Office of Management and Budget. 2003. *Historical Tables, Budget of the United States Government*, http://www.white house.gov/omb/ budget/fy2004/pdf/hist.pdf (accessed October 4, 2005).

U.S. Social Security Administration. 2002. Memorandum from Stephen Goss to Daniel Patrick Moynihan, January 31, http:// www.ssa.gov/OACT/solvency/PresComm_20020131.html (accessed October 4, 2005).

———. 2004. Social Security Quick Calculator. In *Social Security Online*, July 9, http://www.ssa.gov/OACT/quickcalc/calculator .html (accessed July 11, 2005).

van IJzendoorn, M., F. Juffer, and C. Poelhuis. 2005. Adoption and Cognitive Development: A Meta-Analytic Comparison of Adopted And Nonadopted Children's IQ and School Performance. *Psychological Bulletin* 131 (2): 301–16.

Walzer, M. 1983. *Spheres of Justice: A Defense of Pluralism and Equality.* New York: Basic Books.

Wilson, J. Q. 1993. *The Moral Sense.* New York: The Free Press.

About the Author

Charles Murray is the W. H. Brady Scholar in Culture and Freedom at the American Enterprise Institute for Public Policy Research in Washington, D.C. He is the author of eight other books, including *Losing Ground*, *The Bell Curve* (with Richard J. Herrnstein), and *Human Accomplishment*.

Index

Energy, Department of, 137t.
Europe, 55, 96, 102, 112
  as welfare states, 1, 3, 83–87
Europe Syndrome, 84–87

Family, more autonomous and
    responsible, 107–9
Farmers, 132, 160
Fathers, unwed, 63–64, 70, 102
Favored groups, 17, 132–38,
    144–46
Fertility rates, 85, 191n.3
Florence Crittendon Homes,
    118–19
Food stamps, 17, 56–57, 187n.6
Ford Foundation, 120
Four percent return on invest-
    ments, 26–30, 34–36,
    162–63, 176
France, 83, 191n.3
Fraternal associations, 113–15
Friedman, Milton, 8–9

Germany, 27, 83, 182n.12,
    191n.3
Grant ($10,000), 10, 12, 14, 15
  effects of age of beginning,
    75–79
  health-care portion, 51
  payback point of, 75
  retirement portion, 31, 51
Great Society, 113
Gross domestic product growth,
    125–26
Guaranteed, universal, mini-
    mum income, 10, 15, 30

Happiness
  definition of, 87–88

pursuit of, 82–83
  raw materials for, 88–90
Health care
  affordable, 50–51
  falling real costs of, 38–40
  quality of, 38
  reforms needed, 43–50
  soaring costs, reasons for,
    40–43
Health insurance
  employer-provided as taxable
    income, 47–48
  market, 184n.7
  for those in midlife, 197n.5
  universally required, 45–47
Housewives, full time, 72,
    105–6
Housing and Urban Develop-
    ment, Department of,
    136t.
Human nature, and success of
    the Plan, 91–94

Immigrants, 16, 178n.2
Incarcerated criminals, 16,
    178n.2
Indiana, 9
Industry, see Corporate welfare
Inequality of wealth, 4–5
  solution to, 1, 5
Insurance
  health/medical, see Health
    insurance
  by voluntary associations,
    113–14, 116–17
Insurers, health/medical, 44–47
Interior, Department of, 136t.
Iowa, 8
Italy, 191n.3

increases in costs of, 18–19
Middle-income households
    transition costs, 159–61,
    169–72
Minneapolis, 183n.2
MinuteClinic, 183n.2
Moose, 113
Moral hazard, 117–19
Mothers
    easier to have both children
    and career under the Plan,
    104–5
    easier to stay home under the
    Plan, 105–7
    single, 57–58, 97, 157
    teenage, 62

National Association of Trial
    Lawyers, 49
National Fraternal Congress,
    113–14
Nature of man, and success of
    the Plan, 90–94
Negative income tax, 8–9, 74,
    79, 192n.3
Netherlands, 2, 83, 191n.3
New Hampshire Bureau of
    Labor, 114
New Jersey, 9
New York City
    poverty in, in 1900, 115–16
    school staffs, 194n.14
    social services in by churches,
    114–15
Nonprofit groups, see Favored
    groups

Odd Fellows, 113, 114
Off-the-book jobs, 190n.3

Passport, 10
Pell Grants, 78
Pennsylvania, 9
Philanthropies, private, 115,
    118–19
Plan, the
    and affordable health care,
    50–51
    costs of, see Costs of the Plan
    vs. current system for low-
    income college students,
    78–79
    description of, 9–14
    effects on civil society, 117,
    123–24
    effects on retirement, 24–36
    and job-related medical and
    retirement benefits, 97
    and marriage, 101–10
    and nature of man, 90–94
    political feasibility of, 125,
    157–58, 173
    potential effect on work, 72–73
    provides a stake, opportunity
    to realize ambitions, 70–71,
    98–100
    real purpose of, 94
    reasons for inevitability of,
    125–27
    tax rates and after-tax income
    under (compared with cur-
    rent system), 148–56
    would regenerate voluntary
    associations and their chari-
    ties, 117, 123–24
Plan B (retirement account),
    31–34, 53, 58
Political feasibility of the Plan,
    125, 157–58, 173

Board of Trustees

Bruce Kovner, *Chairman*
Chairman
Caxton Associates, LLC

Lee R. Raymond,
Vice Chairman
Chairman and CEO, Retired
Exxon Mobil Corporation

Tully M. Friedman, *Treasurer*
Chairman and CEO
Friedman Fleischer & Lowe LLC

Gordon M. Binder
Managing Director
Coastview Capital, LLC

Harlan Crow
Chairman and CEO
Crow Holdings

Christopher DeMuth
President
American Enterprise Institute

Morton H. Fleischer
Chairman
Spirit Finance Corporation

Christopher B. Galvin
Chairman
Harrison Street Capital, LLC

Raymond V. Gilmartin
Special Advisor to the
Executive Committee
Merck & Co., Inc.

Harvey Golub
Chairman and CEO, Retired
American Express Company

Robert F. Greenhill
Chairman and CEO
Greenhill & Co.

Roger Hertog

Martin M. Koffel
Chairman and CEO
URS Corporation

John A. Luke Jr.
Chairman and CEO
MeadWestvaco Corporation

L. Ben Lytle
Chairman and CEO
AXIA Health Management, LLC

Robert A. Pritzker
President and CEO
Colson Associates, Inc.

J. Joe Ricketts
Chairman and Founder
Ameritrade Holding Corporation

Kevin B. Rollins
President and CEO
Dell Inc.

Edward B. Rust Jr.
Chairman and CEO
State Farm Insurance Companies

The American Enterprise Institute
for Public Policy Research

Founded in 1943, AEI is a nonpartisan, nonprofit research
and educational organization based in Washington, D.C.
The Institute sponsors research, conducts seminars and
conferences, and publishes books and periodicals.

AEI's research is carried out under three major programs: Economic Policy Studies; Foreign Policy and
Defense Studies; and Social and Political Studies.
The resident scholars and fellows listed in these pages
are part of a network that also includes ninety adjunct
scholars at leading universities throughout the United
States and in several foreign countries.

The views expressed in AEI publications are those of
the authors and do not necessarily reflect the views of
the staff, advisory panels, officers, or trustees.

Mel Sembler
Founder and Chairman
The Sembler Company

William S. Stavropoulos
Chairman
The Dow Chemical Company

Wilson H. Taylor
Chairman Emeritus
CIGNA Corporation

James Q. Wilson
Pepperdine University

Emeritus Trustees

Willard C. Butcher

Richard B. Madden

Robert H. Malott

Paul W. McCracken

Paul F. Oreffice

Henry Wendt

Officers

Christopher DeMuth
President

David Gerson
Executive Vice President

Jason Bertsch
Vice President, Marketing

Henry A. Olsen III
Vice President
Director of the National Research
Initiative

Danielle Pletka
Vice President, Foreign and Defense
Policy Studies

Council of Academic
Advisers

James Q. Wilson, *Chairman*
Pepperdine University

Eliot A. Cohen
Professor and Director of Strategic
Studies
School of Advanced International
Studies
Johns Hopkins University

Gertrude Himmelfarb
Distinguished Professor of History
Emeritus
City University of New York

Samuel P. Huntington
Albert J. Weatherhead III
University Professor of Government
Harvard University

William M. Landes
Clifton R. Musser Professor of Law
and Economics
University of Chicago Law School

Sam Peltzman
Ralph and Dorothy Keller
Distinguished Service Professor
of Economics
Graduate School of Business
University of Chicago

Nelson W. Polsby
Heller Professor of Political Science
Institute of Government Studies
University of California–Berkeley

George L. Priest
John M. Olin Professor of Law and
Economics
Yale Law School

Jeremy Rabkin
Professor of Government
Cornell University

Murray L. Weidenbaum
Mallinckrodt Distinguished
University Professor
Washington University

Richard J. Zeckhauser
Frank Plumpton Ramsey Professor
of Political Economy
Kennedy School of Government
Harvard University

Research Staff

Gerard Alexander
Visiting Scholar

Joseph Antos
Wilson H. Taylor Scholar in Health
Care and Retirement Policy

Leon Aron
Resident Scholar

Claude E. Barfield
Resident Scholar; Director, Science
and Technology Policy Studies

Roger Bate
Resident Fellow

Walter Berns
Resident Scholar

Douglas J. Besharov
Joseph J. and Violet Jacobs
Scholar in Social Welfare Studies

Edward Blum
Visiting Fellow

Dan Blumenthal
Resident Fellow

Karlyn H. Bowman
Resident Fellow

John E. Calfee
Resident Scholar

Charles W. Calomiris
Visiting Scholar

Lynne V. Cheney
Senior Fellow

Steven J. Davis
Visiting Scholar

Veronique de Rugy
Research Fellow

Thomas Donnelly
Resident Fellow

Nicholas Eberstadt
Henry Wendt Scholar in Political
Economy

Mark Falcoff
Resident Scholar Emeritus

Gerald R. Ford
Distinguished Fellow

John C. Fortier
Research Fellow

Ted Frank
Resident Fellow; Director,
AEI Liability Project

David Frum
Resident Fellow

Ted Gayer
Visiting Scholar

Reuel Marc Gerecht
Resident Fellow

Newt Gingrich
Senior Fellow

James K. Glassman
Resident Fellow

Jack L. Goldsmith
Visiting Scholar

Robert A. Goldwin
Resident Scholar Emeritus

Michael S. Greve
John G. Searle Scholar

Robert W. Hahn
Resident Scholar; Director,
AEI-Brookings Joint Center
for Regulatory Studies

Kevin A. Hassett
Resident Scholar; Director,
Economic Policy Studies

Steven F. Hayward
F. K. Weyerhaeuser Fellow

Robert B. Helms
Resident Scholar; Director,
Health Policy Studies

Frederick M. Hess
Resident Scholar; Director,
Education Policy Studies

R. Glenn Hubbard
Visiting Scholar

Frederick W. Kagan
Resident Scholar

Leon R. Kass
Hertog Fellow

Jeane J. Kirkpatrick
Senior Fellow

Herbert G. Klein
National Fellow

Marvin H. Kosters
Resident Scholar Emeritus

Irving Kristol
Senior Fellow Emeritus

Desmond Lachman
Resident Fellow

Michael A. Ledeen
Freedom Scholar

Adam Lerrick
Visiting Scholar

James R. Lilley
Senior Fellow

Lawrence B. Lindsey
Visiting Scholar

John R. Lott Jr.
Resident Scholar

John H. Makin
Visiting Scholar

N. Gregory Mankiw
Visiting Scholar

Allan H. Meltzer
Visiting Scholar

Joshua Muravchik
Resident Scholar

Charles Murray
W. H. Brady Scholar

Roger F. Noriega
Visiting Fellow

Michael Novak
George Frederick Jewett Scholar
in Religion, Philosophy, and Public
Policy; Director, Social and Political
Studies

Norman J. Ornstein
Resident Scholar

Richard Perle
Resident Fellow

Alex J. Pollock
Resident Fellow

Sarath Rajapatirana
Visiting Fellow

Michael Rubin
Resident Scholar

Sally Satel
Resident Scholar

Gary Schmitt
Resident Scholar

Joel Schwartz
Visiting Fellow

Vance Serchuk
Research Fellow

Daniel Shaviro
Visiting Scholar

Christina Hoff Sommers
Resident Scholar

Phillip L. Swagel
Resident Scholar

Samuel Thernstrom
Managing Editor, AEI Press;
Director, W. H. Brady Program

Fred Thompson
Visiting Fellow

Peter J. Wallison
Resident Fellow

Scott Wallsten
Resident Scholar

Ben J. Wattenberg
Senior Fellow

John Yoo
Visiting Scholar

Karl Zinsmeister
J. B. Fuqua Fellow; Editor,
The American Enterprise